WHAT THEY DIDN'T TEACH YOU IN GRADUATE SCHOOL

WHAT THEY DIDN'T TEACH YOU IN GRADUATE SCHOOL

199 Helpful Hints for Success in Your Academic Career

PAUL GRAY and DAVID E. DREW

Foreword by *Laurie Richlin*
Foreword by *Steadman Upham*
Cartoons by *Matthew Henry Hall*

STERLING, VIRGINIA

Published by Stylus Publishing, LLC
22883 Quicksilver Drive
Sterling, Virginia 20166–2102

Library of Congress Cataloging-in-Publication Data
Gray, Paul, 1930–
    What they didn't teach you in graduate school : 199 helpful hints for new and future faculty on how to succeed in academe / Paul Gray and David E. Drew ; forewords by Laurie Richlin and Steadman Upham ; cartoons by Matthew Henry Hall.—1st ed.
        p.   cm.
    Includes bibliographical references.
    ISBN 978–1-57922–264–2 (pbk. : alk. paper)
    1. College teaching—Vocational guidance—United States.   2. College teachers—United States.   3. First year teachers—United States.   I. Drew, David E.   II. Title.
LB1778.2.G73 2008
378.1'202373—dc22

                                                                                        2007025432

13-digit ISBN: 978–1–57922–264–2 (paper)

Printed in the United States of America

All first editions printed on acid free paper
that meets the American National Standards Institute
Z39–48 Standard.

Bulk Purchases

Quantity discounts are available for use in workshops
and for staff development.
Call 1–800–232–0223

First Edition, 2008

10   9   8   7   6   5   4   3   2   1

To all the new PhD's and about-to-be PhD's
who will read this book.

To the memory of Belle Epstein Drew
1919–2002
and to Alane

David Drew

To my wife, Muriel

Paul Gray

The authors and Stylus Publishing, LLC acknowledge *Inside Higher Ed* and a number of doctoral seminars for providing forums in which to present a number of these hints. The authors thank Ms. Teresa Wilborn for her help in preparing the manuscript.

CONTENTS

CHAPTER FIVE: RESEARCH

CHAPTER SIX: TENURE

CHAPTER TEN: DIVERSITY

CHAPTER ELEVEN: ON WRITING

CHAPTER TWELVE: ON PUBLISHING

CHAPTER THIRTEEN:
PERSONAL CONSIDERATIONS

CHAPTER FOURTEEN: FINAL THOUGHTS

CHAPTER FIFTEEN:
CONCLUSION AND ENVOI

APPENDIXES
APPENDIX A: THE DISSERTATION

APPENDIX D: YOUR HEALTH

FOREWORD 1

What I Wished I Had Known

OR 20 YEARS I HAVE WORKED with faculty members at all types of institutions, from small colleges through large universities, on how to design their courses to facilitate, assess, and document learning. During that time I also have taught hundreds of graduate students interested in an academic career. Although professors are deeply concerned about their subjects, their students' learning, and their institutions' culture, most receive no preparation to deal with the complex issues involved in being a faculty member. This lack of understanding is doubly true for graduate students preparing for academic careers. Of course, neither group should be expected to know how to become or be a faculty member: In almost all cases no one ever taught them how to improve learning or participate in campus governance. Just as teachers do not expect students to learn how to perform complex tasks without study, practice, and feedback, faculty members cannot be effective academic citizens or instructors without similar processes.

I long ago realized what a particularly lucky person I was to receive my committee's guidance to complete my doctoral program and move into a university career. Since then, as I have researched graduate student advising and mentoring, I have found that across graduate programs and institutions, students report uncertainty about deciding on dissertation topics, finding an academic job, and what will be required of them to be a success as a professor. What distinguishes this book is that it provides, in one place, the guidance and the help that graduate students and faculty members need to achieve their professional goals.

What I find useful about this book is that Gray and Drew approach faculty work as a job as well as a career. The ideas apply equally to experienced, veteran faculty members and to the graduate students I teach in my university's Preparing Future Faculty Program. They make it clear that being a scholar means more than loving your subject. Through their wry "hints," they guide the reader behind the scenes to

- GRADUATE SCHOOL: a short time in the course of an academic career (we hope), but a busy one for survivorship (Hint 9: *Remember that a Ph.D. is primarily an indication of survivorship*); finding mentors (2: *Most academic fields are dominated by fewer than one hundred powerful people*); getting known (6: *Specialize*); and, most of all, finishing (13: *Be aware that the key danger point in any doctoral program is the one where you leave highly structured coursework [Phase I] and enter the unstructured world of the qualification examination and the dissertation [Phase II]*).
- FINDING A JOB: a research process that begins almost the first day of graduate school, and involves everything from a lifestyle choice (18: *Pick a place where you and your family want to live*) to understanding disciplinary "supply and demand."
- PUBLISHING: Most important is Drew's Law that every study can be published somewhere (Hint 4) and Gray's Theorem that tenure requires $n + 2$ publications where $n =$ the number you

have (Hint 1). Publishing also requires learning how to write (*129: Be sure to spell check [and grammar check and fact check] your work*); how to negotiate the publishing world (*135: Submit your papers [other than those you know are stinkers] first to the best journals in the field; 141: As an author, you don't help matters if you take a long time between receiving reviews and submitting the revised manuscript;* and *143: As they say in Chicago, publish early and often*) and other editorial and writing hints

- TEACHING AND SERVICE: being a good teacher (*39: Teaching is a great personal satisfaction and an important public good that you perform*) and academic citizen (*79: Never, ever choose sides in department politics; 86. Join the faculty club; 104: Get to know the people in Development and support them*) may not be what many graduate students think about when choosing the professorial career, but, as the authors point out, both make a big impact on success at an institution

- ADMINISTRATION: Gray and Drew deal forthrightly with administration (*76: Administrators usually are paid more than professors.*); the challenges of the usual first step, becoming a department chair (*108: Never, never become a department chair, even an acting department chair, unless you are a tenured full professor; 114: If you are department chair, don't stay in the job too long*); and the possibility of joint administration and teaching appointments leading to the tenure track (*27: If your field is one in which there is an oversupply of people, one strategy is to seek a job as an Assistant Dean*).

- TENURE AND PROMOTION: This is the goal toward which the new academics point their work. The special sections on tenure and academic rank, in particular, provide the straightforward set of recommendations no one else will give you. Tenure (*58: Don't count on a grant or contract until you receive the signed letter of approval; 61: The tenure clock is really four and a half years, not seven; 63: If, by chance, you are tenured, never take another appointment without it)* and Academic Rank (*69: Being a tenured full professor in a research university is as close to freedom as you can come in U.S. society; 71: Avoid becoming the dreaded "Permanent Associate Professor"*).

Gray and Drew include appendixes on the dissertation, outside income, writing hints, and—very importantly—health considerations for facing the rigors of an academic job.

This book is full of wonderful, witty, and, of course, true suggestions from two experienced mentors about the academic career.

Finally, I propose an additional hint for those who wish to become superb professors:

200: *Read this book.*

Laurie Richlin
Director of the Claremont Graduate University Preparing
Future Faculty & Learning Communities Program
Claremont, California

FOREWORD 2

WILL NEVER FORGET MY FIRST DAY of graduate school at Arizona State University in 1976. I entered the west door of the Anthropology Building after parking in the small lot that I later learned was reserved for the department's full professors. Down a half flight of stairs and there I was, thrust into a series of winding hallways and closed doors that held faculty offices, archaeology labs, storage rooms, graduate assistant cubicles, and the office of the archaeology laboratory supervisor (and the most important person for me during that first year), Mrs. Laughlin.

My journey toward the PhD had begun, and my profoundest memories of those first few months center not on the subjects I was studying, but on the closed and locked doors in the anthropology building. I knew that behind each door was a professor I did not know, a new body of knowledge I wanted to learn, new graduate student colleagues I wished to meet, exotic collections of artifacts I would eventually study, and various tools of the trade with which I was unfamiliar (laser transits, magnetometers, and the peculiar aluminum cubes used to take samples for archaeomagnetic dating). Slowly, over the course of four and a half years, I would gain access to each of those doors in the anthropology building, and to the treasures, challenges, and curiosities that formed my path to both a master's degree and PhD in anthropology and archaeology.

Mrs. Laughlin was my first guide to graduate school during those formative months. She informed me of lab protocols, advised me about the personality quirks of various professors, steered me to key resources in the library and special collections, and was a kind of confidante after class grades were given and feelings were bruised. But most importantly, Mrs. Laughlin held the keys to all of the locked doors in the archaeology wing of the building, and it was through Mrs. Laughlin that I began to gain access to the spaces and tools of archaeology at ASU.

What They Didn't Teach You in Graduate School provides the same kind of crucial information for graduate students that I gleaned from Mrs. Laughlin. There is an unwritten code of conduct for graduate students, and there are many rules of the road that can be learned only from someone who has taken the journey. Professors Gray and Drew do a remarkable job of delivering both the code and the rules, and they do so with wit, insight, humor, and the voice of experience. This is not surprising, since Paul Gray and David Drew are consummate academics—award-winning teachers, world-class researchers, and the kind of colleagues that make for valued and lifelong friends.

More importantly, Gray and Drew go well beyond the graduate student years to offer counsel and advice to beginning faculty members about the mysteries of university life. Their hints and aphorisms provide a priceless guide to the sometimes odd, unpredictable, and counterintuitive culture of academe. Gray and Drew explain the intricacies of faculty life, discuss the all-important quality of collegiality, and reflect on great teaching and the conduct of significant research. Several of the issues they highlight are worth noting.

First is mentoring. One simply cannot overestimate the importance of a mentor. Often, we tend to think of mentoring as something that is done to us while we are graduate students. But Gray and Drew point out how mentors are important for each of us at every stage of our career. And as one receives mentoring, even as a faculty member, it is vital for faculty to keep the chain of support intact by mentoring graduate students and junior colleagues in the department.

Second are indisposition and procrastination. Many pitfalls dot the path to a higher degree, or to tenure and promotion. Watson's Syndrome (Hint 15) has derailed more graduate students and wrecked more academic careers than any other single cause I can think of. I have seen it time and time again during the 30-plus years I have spent in academe. Never-ending literature reviews and eternal computer runs to crunch the last bit of life out of a data set are excuses for not drawing conclusions or taking a position on an important issue. As Gray and Drew point out, such frailties will be quickly noted by more experienced academics, and presage an early exit from academe.

Third is computers. Digital resources are not just important to your academic career, they are absolutely vital (see Hints 95 through 103). Digital tools enhance productivity and are the currency of communication with today's students. You can choose to be a Luddite, but if you do you will be standing in the unemployment line still wondering if the best fountain pens are made by Delta or Waterman.

Finally, and of greatest importance to me, is the fundamental message of this book: Value erudition and celebrate enlightened understanding! Gray and Drew make it clear that they "consider Professor to be the best job available on the planet," and universities to be "wonderful, and occasionally transcendent, places to work." I heartily agree with this assessment. These qualities flow from a community of scholars that is organized around the love and pursuit of knowledge. *What They Didn't Teach You in Graduate School* is a guide to this astonishing world, and a most useful and entertaining primer on how to be successful and happy in academe. I only wish I had had a copy of this book on my first day of graduate school so many years ago.

Steadman Upham
The University of Tulsa
Tulsa, Oklahoma

INTRODUCTION

G RADUATE SCHOOL IS A WONDERFUL, heady time for students, particularly those working toward the highest achievement, the PhD. It is a time when long-term friendships are formed. It is a time when the discussion in seminars, in classes, and with other graduate students focuses on the intellectual life. Yes, there are financial worries, given the expenses and the low pay. Yes, there are the problems of maturing for students fresh out of undergraduate school and the problems of reentering academia after a long time away for students over 30. Nonetheless, it is a marvelous time in your life, and one that you, like today's professors, will look back at fondly.

When you receive the degree and find your first job, you will be exposed to the realities of academic life. What will it be like? How should I navigate this particular real world I am thrust into? Most students, even those who taught part-time before their degree, have only the vaguest concepts of that world. It is the purpose of this book to reduce the uncertainty, to present an irreverent guide to what it is *really* like, at least as seen by the two authors who each spent a long time immersed in this world as well as in the world outside academia.

We deliberately kept this book short, by presenting it in the form of 199 "hints" about what no one told you in graduate school but what you really need to know. Some of the hints are short, others longer. Some of the individual hints are worthy of chapters or books of their own whereas others are important tidbits to tuck into your head for future reference. We've tried to write the hints with a bit of humor here and there. Don't be put off by that. What we say is indeed true, to the best of our knowledge

Since we suspect you will keep this book and keep referring to it as you face new situations, we've organized the hints into 15 short chapters and 4 appendixes: the dissertation, outside income, writing hints, your health.

This book is written in terms of our experience in the United States. That is the universe we know. We recognize that procedures, rules, and assumptions differ by country, even those as close as Canada and Mexico. If you are outside the United States and are reading this book, please pardon our parochialism.

Our hints are based on what we see today in the world around us. It does not reflect the way we think academia should be or could be. Unfortunately, or fortunately, depending on your point of view, academia moves slowly. Therefore, much of what is in this book will stand you in good stead for a considerable fraction of your career. Changes are in the wind that may affect you. For example, many argue that tenure will not be here forever. Yet, in the short term, you will need to deal with it, and we included a chapter about it.

A particular reality of academia is that, in a number of fields, jobs for fresh PhDs are scarce. Although you don't like to think about it in pure business terms, the market for PhDs depends on supply and demand, and is notoriously difficult to model and predict. Students make decisions about the field they want to enter years before they complete their degree. Hence you play a futures game in a changing environment. We do know, however, to use that tired cliché, what goes out of fashion comes back into fashion.

Be aware that the authors of this book come from a research institution that, like them, values teaching highly. We observe that those with strong research productivity are hired for the most prized and best-paid positions in higher education. We also observe that many new PhDs see teaching as their highest calling and want to spend their life at it. Fortunately, the largest employers of faculty are the four-year and community colleges that value teaching first.

In this book we talk not only about the mechanics of being a professor but the nature of life as an academic. The next five paragraphs present our view of that life.

At any given college or university, life is divided arbitrarily into semesters or quarters. For convenience, we will talk in terms of semesters. Even at the smallest of schools, at the beginning of each semester you (and your students) face new students whom you've never seen before and many of whom you will never see again in class. Classes meet on a heartbeat schedule—for example, Monday, Wednesday, and Friday for one hour—for a fixed number of weeks. Then it is all over and you start again. After the spring semester, if you don't teach summer school, you are free to do what you want. For most academics summer becomes a time to prepare for the next academic year and to do research and, perhaps, take some vacation. But summer is soon over and you start again.

Whereas students change from semester to semester, your faculty colleagues change only slowly. Yes, some people move on or retire and new people are brought in to take their place (just as you were), but tomorrow's faculty is like today's faculty, only slightly different. They are people you must live with and who must live with you over considerable periods of time. Then there's the administration and the staff, who, like your colleagues, also change only slowly.

With few exceptions, when you take your first job you are off to a new school, one often distant from where you formed those strong friendships and learned your profession. Many PhDs starting out find that they are the only ones in their department who are deep into their specialty within their field. After all, it was your specialty you were hired for.

You will spend a considerable part of your first year just learning about the school and its norms, establishing a social network of people you are compatible with and whom you trust, and preparing the courses you are assigned to teach. If in a research-intensive school, you are also expected to advance your research; if in a teaching institution, your teaching load is heavier and you serve on more committees. You also learn about the quality of the students you teach.

It is a good life, and you even get paid.

Many universities offer Preparing Future Faculty (PFF) programs for PhD students.[1] The objective of these programs is essentially the same as this book. If your university offers such a program, enroll! You will learn much that is vital for success as a professor. We are such fans of our university's PFF program that we asked its director, Laurie Richlin, to write one of the forewords for this book.

We've enjoyed writing these hints and hope that you will find them useful. We look forward to receiving feedback from you, both favorable and unfavorable, confirming or disconfirming our advice. We hope you will send us new hints, including ideas that we left out, so that we can include them in future editions for future PhDs. We will, of course, credit you for your input.

Paul Gray (paul.gray@cgu.edu) David E. Drew (david.drew@cgu.edu)
Claremont, California
August 2007

---

[1] The name may differ from school to school. The objective, however, is the same: to tell PhD students about the world they are about to enter.

1

BASIC CONCEPTS

HINT 1: GRAY'S THEOREM OF $N + 2$. The number of papers required for tenure is $N + 2$, where N is the number you published.

EACH YEAR, PHD CANDIDATES AND young faculty members come into our offices and sheepishly ask us to tell them what they really need to know about building a career in academia. We usually take them to a long lunch and give them the helpful hints that we share with you in this book.

1. GRAY'S THEOREM OF $N + 2$. The number of papers required for tenure is $N + 2$, where N is the number you published.

    Corollary: Gray's Theorem is independent of N.

2. MOST ACADEMIC FIELDS ARE DOMINATED by fewer than 100 powerful people. These people know one another and determine the course of the field. Early in your career you should get to know as many of them as possible. More to the point, they should know who you are. You want them to see you as a bright young person at the forefront of your field. Although this tactic is important, be aware of the dangers associated with it. You should not begin the process until after you mastered the literature (particularly the papers they wrote!) and developed some ideas of your own. If they get to know you and conclude you have no ideas, you're finished.

3. THINK OF WHOM YOU KNOW IN THE FIELD:

- People who write books
- People who publish papers
- People active in their professional societies

    Use this list as a guide for deciding what you can do to become one of the *known people*.

4. DREW'S LAW. Every paper can be published somewhere. Your first papers will be rejected. Don't worry about this. View the reviewer's complete misunderstanding of your brilliance as cheap editorial help. Use his or her advice to revise. Every paper has a market. If *Journal A* rejects it, make the appropriate changes and send it to *Journal B*. If the work is sound, someone will publish it.

5. MAKE SURE YOU HAVE A MENTOR early in your career. The old apprentice system still exists. Try to find mentors who were successful with others, who will support you, and who believe that furthering your career helps their own career. Such a mentor is preferable to the internationally famous Nobel Prize winner who exploits you.

6. SPECIALIZE. Get known for something. It helps visibility. Sadly, brilliant, restless people who work on several topics simultaneously usually do not achieve as much visibility as those who plod along in the same area for many years.

2

THE PhD

List of Things To Do
(Besides Work on Dissertation)

1. Make List of Things To Do (Besides Work on Dissertation).
2. Stare Blankly At List.
3. Stare Blankly Out Window.
4. Repeat #2 & #3 For Several Hours.
5. Go Out For Walk or Bike Ride. (You Deserve a Break!)
6. On Walk/Bike Ride Get Long Series of Brilliant Ideas for Dissertation.
7. Curse Yourself For Not Bringing Anything To Write Brilliant Ideas Down With Or On.
8. Continue to Be Mad At Yourself When You Get Home For Not Remembering Any Of Your Brilliant Ideas For Your Dissertation Because You Got So Upset At Yourself For Not Bringing Anything To Write Brilliant Ideas Down With Or On.
9. Repeat #7 & #8 For Several Hours.
10. Resolve Finally To Change!
11. Make List of Pens, Paper, Notebooks of All Sizes, New Backpack, Organizer, Folders, More Pens, More Paper.
12. Go To Office Supply Store.
13. Forget to Bring Wallet.
14. Curse Self For Forgetting Wallet.
15. Go Back Home.
16. Add "New Wallet With Chain" To List. (Over)

HINT 15: AVOID WATSON'S SYNDROME
. . . a euphemism for procrastination.

I T CAN BE ARGUED THAT YOU DO JOB HUNTING (the subject of chapter 3) before you receive the PhD. However, the PhD is the prize you seek above all from your graduate experience. We therefore discuss it first.

7. FINISH YOUR PHD AS EARLY AS POSSIBLE. Don't feel that you need to create the greatest work that Western civilization ever saw. Five years from now the only thing that will matter is whether you finished. If you don't finish, you are likely to join the ranks of "freeway flyers," holding multiple part-time teaching jobs.

8. BE HUMBLE ABOUT YOUR PHD. You don't need to flaunt the degree. Everyone has one. Many of your colleagues, both in your institution and outside it, will be put off if you sign everything "Doctor" or "Jane Jones, PhD" In fact, the main use for Doctor is making reservations at a restaurant. When you call and ask for a table for four for Doctor Jones, you will get more respect and often better seating.

9. REMEMBER THAT A PHD IS PRIMARILY an indication of survivorship. Although the public at large may view your doctorate as a superb intellectual achievement and a reflection of brilliance, you probably know deep in your heart that it is not. It represents a lot of hard work on your part over a long period of time. You probably received help from one or more faculty to get over rough spots. Your family, be it parents or spouse, stayed with you over the vicissitudes of creating the dissertation. You stuck with it until it was done, unlike the ABDs (All But Dissertation), people who complete all the other requirements but bail out before they finish their dissertations.

10. A PHD IS A CERTIFICATION OF RESEARCH ABILITY based on a sample of 1. The PhD certifies that you are able to do quality research. Unlike the MD, which requires extensive work with patients followed by years of internship and residency, the PhD is based on a single sample, your dissertation. The people who sign your dissertation are making a large bet on your ability to do quality research again and again in the future.

11. A PHD IS A LICENSE TO REPRODUCE and an obligation to maintain the quality of your intellectual descendants. Once you are a PhD, it is possible for you (assuming you are working in an academic department that offers a PhD program) to create new PhDs. Even if your department does not offer a PhD, you can be called upon to sit on PhD examining committees either in your own or in neighboring institutions. This is a serious responsibility because you are creating your intellectual descendants. Recognize that if you vote to pass someone who is marginal or worse, that PhD in turn is given the same privilege. If candidates are not up to standard, it is likely that some of their descendants will also not be. Unlike humans whose intergeneration time is 20 years, academic intergeneration times are 5 years or less. Furthermore, a single individual may supervise 50 or more PhDs over a 30-year career.

12. YOU MUST HAVE THE PHD IN HAND before you can move up the academic ladder. The world is full of ABDs. We talked about them briefly in Hint 9 and will again in Hint 161. ABDs may be much abler and more brilliant than you but they didn't possess the stamina (or the circumstances) to finish the degree. In our judgment, being an ABD is the end of the academic line.

13. BE AWARE THAT THE KEY DANGER POINT in any doctoral program is the one where you leave highly structured coursework (Phase 1) and enter the unstructured world of the qualification examination and the dissertation (Phase 2). Here are two strategies to help you navigate Phase 2:

1. Stay in touch with your professors, especially your adviser. One of us insists that students come in for a meeting each week, even if nothing happened. Just the fear of not being able to report anything stimulates the mind.
2. Meet regularly, ideally every week, for lunch or dinner or afternoon coffee, with two or three fellow graduate students who are also struggling with Phase 2. Compare notes and progress.

14. A SPECIAL NOTE FOR THE PART-TIME STUDENT working on the dissertation. Although all PhD students used to be on campus and often worked as teaching or research assistants part-time, in many fields today that attract midcareer students (for example, education) the norm is to work at an off-campus job full-time and on the PhD part-time. Others, such as computer science students, develop an idea for a start-up company (e.g., one of the founders of Google) and drift from full-time to part-time. We applaud part-time PhD students. This hint is addressed to these students.

If you are working on your PhD part time, you will find it difficult enough in Phase 1 to tell your boss that you can't attend that nighttime budget crisis meeting or tell your spouse that you can't go to your child's soccer game because you must be in class. It is even more difficult when you're in Phase 2 to tell him or her that you won't be there because you must be home, in your study, staring at a blank computer screen trying to get past writer's block.

As a part-time student, you need to find ways (in addition to suggestions 1 and 2 in Hint 13) to be physically present on campus. You can do so in many ways, such as spending time writing in a library carrel.[1] Physical presence is important psychologically. If you never visit campus and become caught up in your work and family activities, you face the danger that your uncompleted PhD program can begin to seem like something you used to do in a faraway time and place.

15. Avoid Watson's Syndrome. Named by R. J. Gelles, this syndrome is a euphemism for procrastination.[2] It involves doing everything possible to avoid completing work. It differs from writer's block in that the sufferer substitutes real work that distracts from doing what is necessary for completing the dissertation or for advancing toward an academic career. The work may be outside or inside the university. Examples given by Gelles include:

- remodeling a house
- a never-ending literature review (after all, new papers are being published all the time and they must be referenced)
- data paralysis—making seemingly infinite Statistical Analysis System (SAS) and Statistical Package for Social Sciences (SPSS) runs
- perfectionism that doesn't let you submit until you think it is perfect (and it never is perfect)

If you suffer from Watson's Syndrome, finding a mentor (see Hint 5) who pushes you to finish will help you get done. For many, however, particularly those who always waited until the night before an examination to begin studying, the syndrome is professionally fatal.

16. CELEBRATE YOUR PHD! When you hand in your signed dissertation and pay the last fee that the university exacts from you, go out and Celebrate! Celebrate! Celebrate! You've achieved something marvelous, and you are one of a very small number in the population who can say you are a PhD. A rough calculation shows that about 3 out of 400 adults in the United States hold a PhD. Attaining a PhD is a big deal! Honor that.

A PhD, like life, is a journey. It marks the end of one stage and the beginning of what lies ahead. Don't fail to appreciate the moment of your accomplishment. Yes, other big moments await you. But like almost every PhD, you never had a moment this big, and it will be a long time before you have another one that matches it.

Notes

1. The library is a large building filled with books and journals. It functions sort of like Google, but deeper.

2. This hint is based on R. J. Gelles, "Watson's Syndrome," *Inside Higher Education*, June 19, 2006, http://www.insidehighered.com/work place/2006/06/19/gelles

3

JOB HUNTING

HINT 29: WHEN INTERVIEWING, try to find out whether the members of the faculty like one another.

THE HINTS IN THIS SECTION ARE directed primarily at those who seek to earn their living in academe. To get in, you must first be offered a job. Your first job will strongly affect the rest of your academic life. If you decide you don't want to go into academe or don't find a job, see Hint 38.

17. JOB HUNTING IS A RESEARCH PROJECT, and you should treat it as such. Gather as much information as possible. Read the ads. Contact sources. Follow up leads. Be aggressive. Use your contacts (see Hint 2). The chance of landing a good appointment is higher if you search broadly than if you sit in your office waiting for one or two possibilities. Begin job hunting early and make it a project you do along with your other work. If you are a graduate student, don't wait until your dissertation is finished to start looking (but see Hint 24).

18. PICK A PLACE WHERE YOU AND YOUR FAMILY want to live and that matches your lifestyle. City people are not happy in isolated college towns and small-city people find it hard to adjust to a megalopolis.

19. TO GET A JOB (AND LATER, TO GET TENURE) you will need references beyond your dissertation committee. Build a reference pool. That is, identify people who will say nice things about you. They needn't be famous or distinguished, but they should hold impressive titles or be employed at prestigious places. References from abroad are particularly desirable since they show you to be a person with some international reputation in your field. Remember that universities are lazy. When references are needed, they will ask you for a long list of names to choose from. Pick your friends.

20. RÉSUMÉS (ALSO CALLED CURRICULUM VITAE, vita, vitae, and CV in academia) are important.[1] They are the entrée to the process. Invest in having yours done professionally. It should be neat but not gaudy. Include everything in your résumé that is remotely relevant. Some search committees use a checklist of skills, experiences, and other criteria they expect for a position. Do you know something about, say, medieval literature or databases, which the department might want you to teach. A committee may blindly drop you from consideration if its members don't put a checkmark next to each of their items. Your problem is that the list of items is different at every institution.

21. WHEN APPLYING FOR A POSITION, interview your potential bosses (e.g., chair, dean) just as they interview you. You will live rather intimately with them for a long time. Make sure you are compatible.

22. IF YOU ARE A NEW PhD OR AN ACTIVE RESEARCHER on a campus visit, many, if not most, of the senior people who interview you produced less, not more, research in the last three years than you did. This is particularly true for older faculty who were granted tenure in easier times. When you are interviewed by such people, be kind. Stress the importance of your research but don't overwhelm them with the details. You don't want them to perceive you as a threat to the comfortable position they now hold.

23. FIND THE BEST POSSIBLE SCHOOL for your first job. You can only go down in the pecking order, not up, if you don't make it at your first position. If you are a success, you can go up one level at a time. Stanford doesn't hire from Winsocki Community College.

24. UNLESS YOU ARE STARVING OR HOMELESS, don't take a tenure-track faculty position without the PhD in hand. We estimate the odds are two to one against your ever finishing your degree. Even if you do finish while on the job, your chances of being tenured go down because you reduced the "seven-year" clock (see Hint 61). Furthermore, without a PhD you will be offered a significantly lower salary and you may never make up the difference. If you must work, the only defense you have is to negotiate with the institution that the clock does not start until you can legitimately be called "Doctor."

25. NONUNIVERSITY RESEARCH ORGANIZATIONS offer the challenge of research without the need or the opportunity to teach. They include industry laboratories, major consulting firms, government laboratories, and not-for-profit think tanks. Each organizatgion has its distinct culture. Many involve military work. In the not-for-profits and the consulting firms, you are only as good as the last contract you brought in. As a result, these organizations experience a high burnout rate among people 45 or older. If you want to go back to academia at some time in the future, you need to create your own portable wealth by publishing (Hint 39). Unfortunately, publishing is counter to the culture in many of these organizations. In some industrial laboratories it is said that if you write $F = ma$ or $E = mc^2$, someone will stamp your report "Company Confidential."

26. AVOID TAKING YOUR FIRST JOB in a school that you attended, no matter how strong your loyalty as an alumnus or alumna. You will always be regarded as a graduate student by the older faculty and will be treated as such. It is different, however, if you leave for some years and then return.

27. IF YOUR FIELD SUFFERS FROM AN OVERSUPPLY of people, one strategy is to seek a job as an assistant dean. This approach is quite tricky. Colleges are always looking for candidates for such necessary but nonglorious jobs as assistant dean for student affairs or assistant dean of administration or assistant dean for summer school. You, as an applicant, should insist that you also receive an appointment (even if not tenure track) in your field of specialty, say, history. You should also insist that you teach one course and that you are given some time for research. Unless you do so, you will never be given a crack at a tenure-track position. You must then be active in your department and be seen by the department as a member in good standing who gives it access to the administration. Even then, you may never be fully accepted (see Hint 80 on joint appointments). However, you will gain experience that can be used later and you will gain the academic title (and the teaching and research experience) needed on your résumé when you look for a job involving full-time teaching and research.

28. THE LAW OF SUPPLY AND DEMAND applies to academia as much as to other fields. You are playing a futures game on the job market, no different from a high roller in the stock market, when you select a field of study for your PhD. Since it takes four to seven years or more to acquire the degree, you make the assumption that your services will be in demand several years from now. They may be, but then again they may not be. Fields move in and out of favor over time. When a hot new field or specialty opens up, it is an exciting time. Lots of people wander in from adjacent fields. They form departments or concentration areas and begin training PhDs in that specialty. People are in short supply and good salaries are offered. However, what usually happens is that within a relatively short period of time, the PhD market becomes saturated and jobs become scarcer. Furthermore, other new specialties emerge and schools cut back on the previous fad. A classic example is operations research (also known as management science). In the 1960s, new departments were formed. By the 1980s, the job market was saturated. In the last decade the supply exceeded the demand, and this in a field that offers industrial as well as academic employment. The obvious implication for graduate students is that fields with an oversupply of applicants make it much harder to obtain either an initial job or tenure. Furthermore, the academic prestige of the school where you will be hired will, on average, be lower and so will the salary.

29. INSTITUTIONS HAVE THEIR OWN CULTURES, and in large institutions, schools and department cultures may also differ. The culture will range from cooperative to cutthroat. Often the culture will change when a new person is appointed president or provost or dean or department chair. That is what makes these appointments so critical to the quality of your life. A cooperative culture should be treasured. It will help you as a young faculty member. Conversely, a cutthroat culture is particularly stressful for young faculty because they come in neither knowing the culture of the place nor being prepared for it. When interviewing, try to find out whether the members of the faculty like one another and try to assess from what they tell you what the cultural norm is. Asking graduate students about faculty infighting won't help because they are usually insulated from it. Remember that, in addition to trying to assess your capabilities and fit with their needs, the interviewers are trying to present as good a picture of themselves as they can so that you will accept their offer should they make one. Thus, always assume that actual conditions are much worse than they are painted during the interview. If you are lucky enough to receive multiple offers, investigate the cultures involved in your choice by speaking to people (if any) you know at the school and to people who recently left it.

30. Two pieces of data about an institution that are important to you are whether you are being offered the right amount of money and what the chances are of your achieving tenure. To this end, obtain information on the salary levels for people in your field. The American Association of University Professors (AAUP) publishes salary averages for many (but not all) colleges. See chapter 8 for more on salary.

31. Tenure levels are a little trickier. First, the number of tenure cases per year in an academic unit tends to be small. You need data for your specialty. However, knowing the tenure fraction for the institution as a whole is also important. If a school tenures 1 in 10 it is a far different place from one that tenures 8 in 10. Just knowing success in the tenure process is not enough. Some schools weed out at the three-year point. Others make tenure so tough that faculty self-destruct by resigning early. Talk with people who recently made tenure in the department. They will usually have the best view of the current situation.

32. Evaluate a postdoc carefully, particularly if you are in the sciences. You should think of a postdoc in cold, hard economic terms. It is an investment (or speculation, depending on your point of view) just like buying stocks or real estate. You will certainly be paid less than if you took a teaching position, but you may gain additional knowledge and experience to make more money in the long run in your chosen field. The anticipated benefits must exceed the short-run costs to make the investment worthwhile. A postdoc is appropriate under the following conditions:

- You are in a field where jobs at good places are scarce and you did not get one or you failed to follow Hint 7 and delayed too long in starting your job search.

- You feel you need to gain specific research tools (or, if a scientist, experience with specialized equipment) to be able to move your research past your PhD dissertation.
- You want to work with a specific individual (preferably one of the powerful 100, see Hint 2) who will further your growth.
- You want to build up your publication list without using up your seven-year clock.

A postdoc is not appropriate if you are afraid of teaching or talking in front of people. You are merely delaying the inevitable. See Hint 42 for help. A postdoc is also not appropriate if you lived on a shoestring for years and/or support a family.

33. IF YOU REALLY WANT A BROADER CHALLENGE, change your career or move every seven years. This advice seems to run counter to our advice to obtain tenure as soon as possible. It is not. As we indicate in Hint 64, tenure can be negotiated on the way in.

Why change?

- It improves salary. People are hired at the national market rate but are given raises based on the internal annual percent increase. Moving is often the only way to maintain parity or to gain a major increase in salary and perquisites.
- It broadens your outlook. Some of it is the Hawthorne effect;[2] people pay attention to you because you are new. In the first few years in the new institution or department you will have the aura of the outside expert. After a while, you are just one of the same old crowd.
- Changing fields allows you to move from a mature area to a new, dynamic one. That's where the fun is. It is also an opportunity to get in on the ground floor of new development. However, you must be careful. Move only to adjacent fields where

you can use most of your tools. Changing careers involves some retooling. Radical swings such as from French to cognitive psychology or electrical engineering are usually impossible without a second PhD.

34. ASK ABOUT THE RETIREMENT SYSTEM when considering an institution. It is really not too early to worry about retirement when interviewing for your first job because it can affect your mobility economically from then on. Recognize that you will most likely be in a state retirement system or in the Teachers Insurance and Annuity Association (TIAA) retirement system. TIAA is subscribed to by most private and some public institutions. In TIAA, once vested (usually, these days, at once) you keep what you have when you move to another institution. State retirement plans are portable within the state but not from one state to another. The major problem comes when you move from a TIAA college to a state institution or the other way around.

35. PARKING

> *"The chancellor's job had come to be defined as providing parking for the faculty, sex for the students, and athletics for the alumni"* Clark Kerr, chancellor of the University of California at Berkeley, 1957

Be sure to inquire about parking because parking can be a big deal. For example, at University of California it is joked that the university is really a parking business that runs its ten campuses only as a way to attract customers. Unless you wind up living a short walk or bike ride from your campus office or living in a city with decent public transportation with stops near your home and your campus, you have little choice but to drive to get to work. If you do, you may be charged a parking fee, usually deducted from your paycheck.

The deduction is from your income and is therefore taxable at your top rate just as your Social Security contribution. Whether you pay a fee or not, all you get is a hunting license to find a space. Some schools do offer reserved parking at an increased fee where "reserved" means that a space is available but not the same one every day. The top fee can be substantial; $750 a year for a reserved space is not uncommon. You can't do much about parking costs except to carpool. But carpooling is difficult because you need to find people who live near you and who are on campus at the same times you are. Be sure to include parking costs in analyzing the true income associated with an offer.

36. REAL PAY. Don't assume that the only relevant dollar number associated with an offer is the total salary. It isn't. What you most need to know is how much money you can spend, how much the spending money can buy, and the quality of life associated with the offer. Here are some considerations:

- Cost of housing. The cost is greater and the size of the home is smaller in, say, Los Angeles than in Cedar Falls, Iowa.
- Cost of living, other than housing. College towns and big cities are generally more expensive to live in but offer more amenities such as theater and activities.
- Quality of schools for your children.
- Local tax structure for sales, state income, and real estate taxes. (Yes, you will make enough money that you need to worry about taxes.)
- Availability of work for your spouse in the community and, of course, the cost of campus parking.

37. GET THE OFFER IN WRITING, including all the detailed promises that were made and agreed upon, as described in Hint 50. Not only do you want the job, but the institution, having decided you are the one, wants you badly. Recognize that the administrators who make the offer may, and often do, lie. Their memory loss when you arrive on campus can far exceed anything that could be expected at their stage of life. They'll tell you that "there must have been a misunderstanding." As we said, get it in writing.

38. YOU MAY FIND AS YOU GO through your job search that you don't really want to work in academe or you may be one of the unlucky ones who doesn't find the right assistant professorship or postdoc or assistant dean's job. In that case, you start to think in terms of finding other employment. The classic case was that of Albert Einstein. In its April 8, 2007, issue in a story on Einstein, the *Los Angeles Times* reported:

> His impudence and lack of deference to authority . . . alienated all of his professors at Zurich Polytechnic. . . . he was the only graduate in his section . . . not offered a junior professorship.[3]

It made his career. A job was found for him at the Swiss Patent Office that gave him time away from the pressures of meeting classes and grinding out research papers so that he could think. The result was Relativity Theory and much more. Eventually he was invited to be a professor.

The point of this story is that innovation and creativity can be gained outside an academic career as much as they can be inside. When you achieve the PhD it is a point of discontinuity in your life when many alternative paths are open to you. The tenure track is only one of them. Life, after all, is what you make of it.

Notes

1. The term vitae or curriculum vitae is preferred in academia, whereas résumé is used more in business. In general, a vitae can be long, whereas a résumé should be succinct.

2. The Hawthorne effect refers to a factory study made between 1924 and 1932 that examined productivity of factory workers when a change was made (such as in light level). The interpretation of the results changed over the years. Today, the Hawthorne effect is taken to mean that paying attention to people results in altering their behavior, regardless of the change. The effect is named for the now defunct Hawthorne plant of Western Electric that was located in Cicero, Illinois. (See Hawthorne effect at http://www.wikipedia.org/wikki/Hawthorneeffect. Retrieved September 2007.)

3. *Los Angeles Times,* http://www.latimes.com/news/opinion/la-op-isaacson8apr08,0,2518121.story?coll = la-opinion-rightrail. Retrieved September 10, 2007.

4

TEACHING AND SERVICE

HINT 43: STUDENTS ARE VERY CONSCIOUS of the amount of money they spend for your class.

ALL FACULTY MEMBERS, whether at a teaching or a research institution, spend a considerable portion of their life in the classroom and involved in service that helps govern the institution. Teaching is a fundamental condition for staying in academe. Furthermore, you may find that teaching and mentoring provide your most rewarding professional experiences. You have the opportunity to make a positive impact on your students' careers and lives.

39. TEACHING IS A GREAT PERSONAL SATISFACTION and an important public good that you perform. However, publications are your only form of portable wealth.

40. SOME PEOPLE WANT TO BE PROFESSORS, love to teach, and believe that research is a necessary evil to get their ticket punched. Without publishing, it is impossible to receive tenure in most schools, particularly research universities. Happily, however, the pendulum has swung. Many colleges, and even some universities now value teaching and reward it on its own merits. But, you better be a "superteacher."

41. TEACHING IS A LEARNED ART. As such it follows a learning curve. Your first effort will not be as good as your second, and your second, in turn, not as good as your third. However, there is a limit on how good you will get. In other words, your teaching ratings will peak and then remain essentially constant. Eventually, you will be bored by the course and your teaching ratings will go down. Don't despair. It is a natural phenomenon. Often it is a result of aging; faculty over 40 relate less and less each year to 18-year-old freshmen if they don't have kids at home. Decreasing teaching ratings are a signal that it is time for you to teach a different course or students at a different level. You may need to strong-arm your department chair, but change you must.

42. GO TO TOASTMASTERS IF YOU NEED TIPS on how to be entertaining and informative in front of a group of students. We have seen it work in many cases. Ignore the fact that Toastmasters attracts mostly business people. The environment gives you privacy.

43. MEETING CLASSES IS PARAMOUNT. Don't cancel classes because it is inconvenient for you to meet them. If, for example, you are out of town attending a national scholarly meeting on a class day, arrange for a colleague to cover for you or arrange a makeup time with the class. If you know far enough in advance when you will be out of town, you can arrange an examination to fall on that day. Be sure it is proctored properly. Missing classes creates more ill will from students than anything else you do. If you miss a lot of classes, even if they are covered by someone else, students will resent you. Students assume that they are taking the class from you, not from a collection of substitutes. In high-tuition institutions (and even in some modest ones) students are very conscious of the amount of money they spend for your class. They will take it out on you on your class ratings. They will complain to the department chair and your colleagues. You will pile up debts to colleagues that you must repay by covering their classes for them. If you repay many such debts, you will lose valuable time from your research and, hence, from your tenure clock.

44. DISTANCE LEARNING IS A BLESSING. Distance learning is a threat. It is a blessing because you can reach students who would otherwise not have the opportunity to learn from you or to savor the beauties of your field. It is a threat because one possible scenario is that colleges and universities will learn that it is cheaper to buy the infrastructure for distance learning than to construct new buildings or to hire new faculty. With distance learning you can instruct (some would say distract) hundreds simultaneously, not just 10 or 30 in your classroom. Also, if you are not a superteacher on video or the Internet, you may not find much of a future market for your services even if you are a great researcher.

45. THE DEATH RATE AMONG AUNTS AND GRANDMOTHERS of college-age students is phenomenal, far beyond anything actuarial. It is skewed toward exam time. A death in the family is the standard excuse for missing classes and examinations. Although some students are remarkably inventive at concocting stories, most are not. Faced with such an excuse, be aware that the student may be working you. These things are also cyclic. If one student gets away with it, others follow, and you face a veritable epidemic among your students' relatives.

46. BELIEVE IT OR NOT, CHEATING IS WIDESPREAD at some undergraduate institutions. If you give tests (particularly if you use the objective Scantron testing forms favored at many colleges), prepare alternative forms and interweave them. Thus, each student who gets Form A is bracketed by two people who receive Form B. Reproduce A and B on different color paper, since students have been known to switch exams. If you are color-blind, make sure the copying staff does not use red or green paper.

47. TEACHING CAN BE A DANGEROUS PROFESSION. It doesn't happen very often, but a student can come into your office or your building and shoot at you or do other physical harm. The 2007 tragedy at Virginia Tech, where a student shot and killed 33 people, including himself, is a poignant example. The cases are sufficiently rare that they are remembered individually. Usually, these incidents are associated with a student failing a class, or a grievance. These admittedly rare tragedies introduce workplace risk into the academic profession. As stated in Hint 90, as a faculty member you are a public person. Your actions affect the lives of real people. Students are prone to the same mental disturbances as people in the society as a whole. A few will be sufficiently unbalanced to take harmful action.

You can reduce your risk by learning about aberrant behavior (e.g., talk to the psychology staff at your campus health service) and by reporting your concerns to the health service and/or the campus police. Be aware of the policy followed in such cases on your campus. Don't try to solve the problem on your own; you may become a target.

48. AVOID SERVING ON A COMMITTEE where you are the technical expert. If you know something about libraries, don't serve on the library committee. If you do, you will be put on the subgroup (or, worse, become the subgroup) to make recommendations or solve the mess in your area of expertise. Such service will eat up enormous amounts of your time with little visible result and even less personal gain for you.

49. OF THE PEOPLE WHO RECEIVE A PhD, the "mode" of the number of manuscripts published is 0 followed closely by 1. That is, if you count how many manuscripts people actually publish, more publish 0 or 1 than any other number. The research also shows that if you publish something while in graduate school, you are much more likely to keep publishing after you finish. If you are a researcher, be thankful for this statistic. It reduces the competition for the limited number of papers that a journal can publish in an issue. If you are a teacher, take solace in these modal values because they show that many other people, like you, value the art of teaching over research.

5

RESEARCH

HINT 53: LEARN GRANTSMANSHIP. . . . Don't be snobbish!

WHETHER YOU GO TO A RESEARCH or a teaching institution, you will want to keep up your research. As we said in Hint 39, teaching is a great personal satisfaction, but research productivity is your prime form of portable wealth.

Doing research is a lot easier if you receive a grant, either from outside or inside the institution. Unfortunately, most novice faculty have no idea how to obtain grants. Therefore, we include six hints on grantsmanship in this chapter.

50. IF YOU WANT A RESEARCH CAREER, make sure that the position you are offered allows you to actually do research. If at all possible, negotiate in advance with your future department chair and dean about your conditions of work. Ask for reduced teaching loads and committee assignments in your first years, seed money for research expenses until you get your grants, equipment (particularly computing equipment), graduate assistants, and more. In particular, obtain a guarantee that you will teach the same courses for the first few years. Your teaching ratings will be better and you will not divert your energies from research by preparing new courses. Since many of these items soak up scarce resources, get them written into your offer letter. If you start out without them it is highly unlikely you will get them later. Even in a tough job market, most of the "goodies" can be negotiated. Once you are selected, especially if you are the first choice, the department is just as hot for you as you are for it.

51. UNDERSTAND THAT YOU CAN TRADE OFF "teaching load" and "research opportunities." The terms themselves speak volumes about the priorities in many leading universities where, unfortunately, low status is accorded to committed and effective teaching. If you do little research, you will not be tenured in a research (i.e., publish-or-perish) institution. If you do even a little research in some teaching institutions, it may be held against you; certainly, if you do a lot of research it will not be considered a good thing. You can tell what kind of institution you are dealing with by examining the teaching load. Four or five 3-unit classes every semester leave most people so exhausted they do not have the energy to do research on any reasonable time scale. They truly carry a "load." In a research institution, teaching is typically two or three courses a semester. Faculty are encouraged to obtain outside funding to support their research activities and to reduce their teaching load. (Note that if you use research funds to reduce teaching time, you will not see a penny of it. The money goes to the institution.) If you intend to do research, seek research opportunities.

52. RESEARCH REQUIRES BOTH QUANTITATIVE and qualitative methods. Each provides different kinds of insights. Be aware that many qualitative researchers consider quantitative types to be mindless empiricists who fail to grasp the subtleties and nuances of the human experience. And many quantitative researchers believe that all true science is quantitative and, furthermore, that qualitative researchers just aren't smart enough to master mathematical techniques. Both these attitudes are ridiculous.

Regardless of your own research style preference, master both qualitative and quantitative methods. If you don't, a Neanderthal on the tenure committee could cast a negative vote.

53. LEARN GRANTSMANSHIP. It is a skill like any other. If necessary, attend special workshops. Educate yourself about who funds your type of research. Don't be snobbish! You may feel deep down that you did not train yourself for a life of the mind in order to become a peddler of slick prose to federal and foundation bureaucrats. But an ability to raise money can have a seismic effect on your career. Simply imagine yourself as one of two finalists for the plum academic position you always dreamed about. Your competitor has a six-hundred-thousand-dollar grant and you don't. What are the odds in your favor?

54. WHEN WRITING A GRANT PROPOSAL:

- Don't be modest. Present the potential contribution of your proposal in the best possible light.
- Keep the budget small or at least reasonable. Remember that funding agencies like sure things, not risks. They'll give a little money to an unknown. For a large amount they'll want one of the powerful 100 (Hint 2) with a track record as a security blanket.
- Provide more details than you think necessary about the procedures you will follow. Your friends and colleagues know that you are skilled at routine procedures, such as questionnaire surveys or statistical analysis, but a skeptical reviewer who has never heard of you needs to be reassured.

55. IF YOUR BRILLIANT GRANT PROPOSAL is declined (foundations never use the word "rejected"), protest! Tell the agency that you understand its limited funds but articulate why the research would have been valuable. It will not change the decision. However, it may pave the way for you to resubmit the idea in the next fiscal year or for you to get favorable treatment on the next one.

If your proposal is declined, ask whether you can obtain a copy of the reviews. Of course, this requires a thick skin. But, you may learn how you can strengthen the proposal for the next time around.

56. WHEN YOU PREPARE A GRANT PROPOSAL, build in an advisory panel of nationally respected experts. (Major think tanks, for example, maintain rosters of such experts, including Nobel Prize winners, who agree to be available for such panels.) Your proposal will be a little more likely to be funded. If it is, you will benefit from the advice of the experts and you will expand your network among the top people in the field. Be careful, however. If a national leader agrees to be listed in three or more of your proposals that are declined, he or she may conclude you are a loser. Shuffle the panels from proposal to proposal.

57. IF YOU GET THE GRANT and you didn't build in an advisory panel, it is not too late to create one to achieve visibility. Once funded, invite some of the leading people in your field to participate on your advisory panel (Hint 2 again). Often you can get them to consult in this way for free or for modest stipends, certainly much less than their outside consulting fee. Your work will benefit from their experience and knowledge. Your visibility will increase significantly.

58. DON'T COUNT ON A GRANT or contract until you receive the signed letter of approval. (Some people say you should wait until you've cashed the first check.) Some government and foundation officials enthusiastically encourage ideas they later decline. They will blame the change, sometimes appropriately, on their external reviewers or on their advisory committee. Remember, things change. Don't believe them until they sign even if they "guarantee" funding for the project.

6

TENURE

HINT 61: THE TENURE CLOCK IS REALLY four and a half years, not seven.

THE MOST DREADED EXPERIENCE for an academic is the tenure process. Without tenure, you cannot stay permanently at an institution as a professor and you must go job hunting in an uncertain market. Some schools may consider it a stain on your record if you tried but failed to obtain tenure. With it, you remove uncertainty.

59. TENURE IS THE PRIZE. Although things are changing, it is still true that tenure is the goal in academia. Many nontenure-track jobs are exciting in higher education and in research organizations, but most new PhDs seeing academic careers want to become tenured professors.[1]

60. UNDERSTAND WHY TENURE IS SUCH A HURDLE. Consider the cost of a positive tenure decision to your institution. Assume for simplicity that you are making $66,666 when up for tenure and will serve the university 30 years after tenure. Assume your academic raises only cover cost of living (the worst case from your point of view, the best from the university's); that is, your salary is nearly the same in real terms for the rest of your career. From your point of view, you certainly think of yourself as worth the $2 million bet the university must make. But think of it from the university's viewpoint. If it awards tenure when it shouldn't, the school made a bad $2 million bet. If it denies tenure to someone and that person many years later wins a Nobel Prize, everyone will conclude, "Old Siwash was stupid." However, that buzz will last only for a few days and the affair will blow over. Although it will cost the school something to hire your replacement if you are denied tenure, with any luck your replacement will work for even less than you did. Any statistician will tell you that, given these upside and downside risks, universities are absolutely rational to err on the no side, not on the yes side.

61. THE TENURE CLOCK IS REALLY four and a half years, not seven. Remember that the rule is that the seventh contracted year is forever. Thus, the latest the tenure decision can be made is in year six. Your dossier must be completed for the powers that be by the beginning of year six. Although you can count publications that are accepted, journal (or book publisher) review time averages more than a year in most fields. Therefore you need to submit your work for publication by the beginning of year five. It will take you six months to write your results. Ergo, four and a half years!

62. TENURE COMMITTEES LOOK ALMOST EXCLUSIVELY at publications that appear in peer-reviewed journals or in scholarly books. It is, in a sense, a tragedy that you get much more credit for what appears in a "write only" journal (i.e., a journal with minute circulation) than for what appears in a high circulation, widely read popular magazine. But that is the way the game is played.

63. IF, BY CHANCE, YOU ACHIEVE TENURE, never take another appointment without it. The people who promise it "real soon" may not be there when the crunch comes. Go to Hint 1.

64. TENURE, LIKE RESEARCH SUPPORT (Hint 50), can be negotiated on the way in. Nobody tells you (and nobody admits it), but tenure is, in effect, transferable. Be firm in your position that you wouldn't think of moving without being tenured in the new institution.

65. New cross-discipline fields are tougher to get tenure in because you are judged by the standards of people who made their mark in a single, well-established discipline. For example, the field of information systems, which is taught in business schools, combines a hard science (computer science) and two soft sciences (organizational behavior and management). People in this field publish at the intersection of disciplines. However, they are judged by people in the pure disciplines and are expected to contribute to these pure disciplines. Research that combines existing ideas from several disciplines is discounted by the purists even though it is the essence of the cross-discipline field.

66. Tenure as we know it today may not be here forever. The problem stems from changes in the retirement law and in public attitudes. Beginning in 1992, you could not be forced to retire because you had reached a mandatory retirement age. Thus, universities that grant tenure are stuck with you as long as you want to work, whether you perform or not. The teaching life is fulfilling and the paycheck is better than your retirement income (your income even gets better if you reach 70½ because you can then take money out of your tax-deferred retirement nest egg and still collect your paycheck as well as your Social Security benefits). Besides, what would you do with yourself in retirement? When our colleague, the late Peter Drucker (who was still teaching at age 92), was asked why he didn't retire, he replied: "Why retire at 65? I can't see myself driving a Winnebago for 25 years."

67. The university's objective is different from yours. It wants to avoid deadwood and take age as prima facie evidence of your being past it. The university certainly wants you out of there before Alzheimer's disease sets in. If the number of positions is constricted, the administration would prefer to take your slot and give it to a bright young person who is more current, may work for less, and who revitalizes your department. Tenure forces a university to hold on to you because firing you because of your age would be discrimination. Younger faculty who want new opportunities generally side with the university. As a result, some universities introduced a "rolling" arrangement where full professors are reviewed every five years and may be encouraged to leave because of poor performance.

Our preliminary indications are that rolling reviews result in making senior people work a little harder. They became professors because they are risk averse and therefore feel that they must now be even more accountable.

68. THE NUMBER OF TENURED SLOTS in some universities may decrease. Jack Schuster and Martin Finkelstein, in a 2006 book on the American professoriate, report data that show that the number of part-time and full-time hires who are off the tenure track increased significantly, from a few percent in the late 1970s to over 50% today.[2] It is not clear whether this change is the result of universities hedging their bets because they fear enrollments will go down in some areas, or whether it is a deliberate move to reduce the size (and with it, the power) of the tenured faculty, or whether they simply want to reduce their payroll.

Notes

1. Both authors worked full time in think tanks after receiving their PhDs prior to beginning their university careers.

2. J. H. Schuster and M. J. Finkelstein, *The American Faculty: The Restructuring of Academic Work and Careers.* Baltimore: Johns Hopkins University Press, (2006).

7

ACADEMIC RANK

HINT 70: To be a full professor,
you must be known for something.

J UST AS THERE HAS BEEN GRADE INFLATION, so has there been rank inflation. It used to be that people with new PhDs were hired as instructors and there were four ranks. Today there are only three, assistant, associate, and full professor. Tenure usually is the transition to associate. Full professor is, of course, the desired state.

69. BEING A TENURED FULL PROFESSOR in a research university is as close to freedom as you can come in U.S. society. Yes, you must meet your classes. However, when you walk into your office in the morning, it is you who decides what you should be working on, not someone else. You can decide to continue what you've done previously or delve into something new. You are limited only by your imagination. It is a state much desired by others and one that you achieved.

70. WHEN YOU REACH THE EXALTED STATE of tenured associate professor, the time has come to see the big picture and undertake large, long-term research projects so that you can become a full professor. Unfortunately, you spent the previous six years (and your dissertation time) doing small, short-term research projects, each designed to earn you a publication or two so that you could achieve tenure. The system never taught you how to conduct a large project. You are therefore put back into a learning situation. Merely doing more of what you did as an assistant professor doesn't hack it in major institutions because the promotion committees ask different questions. Having survived the tenure hurdle, everyone knows you can do research. But to be a full professor, you must be known for something.

71. AVOID BECOMING THE DREADED "Permanent Associate Professor." It is a dead end. You are given all the committee assignments that no one else wants. Although people are nice to Permanent Associate Professors, behind their back they cluck about "poor Smith." It is important for you to remember that if you stay as an associate professor for too long, the time for promotion passes you by. This interval varies from institution to institution. However, while still an assistant, it will pay you to gauge how long it takes people in your school or department to be promoted. Try to be in the middle or earlier. Remember, too, that you must have done something to merit promotion.

72. PROMOTION TO ASSOCIATE PROFESSOR, or from associate to full professor, provides a unique opportunity to request a substantial pay increase. As implied in Hint 33, most universities provide minimal raises for faculty each year. Many make exceptions for a promotion.

8

ACADEMIC SALARY

HINT 76: ADMINISTRATORS USUALLY ARE PAID more than professors. . . . to cope with the stress that comes from the many nasty things they need to do.

Y OU SHOULD NEGOTIATE for the highest initial salary possible because, as we indicated in Hint 33, except for promotion or tenure, you are tied to the average annual raise that the institution gives. This section discusses some of the factors you need to understand.

73. ACADEMICS GENERALLY AVOID RISK. We grant that exceptions exist, but most people going into university teaching are risk averse. They seek security. To them, a dollar at age 70 is as important (or nearly so) as a dollar at age 30. They are willing to take a lower-paying job now because, with tenure, they can expect not to be thrown out on the street at age 50, as happens in industry, with no possibility of finding another job when a reduction in head count takes place. That is, academics have a low discount rate for the future.

74. CONTRACTS ARE GIVEN TO FACULTY for nine months.[1] The other three months are supposedly for you to do with as you please. For example, if you receive, say, $54,000 a year, you are being paid $6,000 a month while working. However, the institution usually pays you in 12 installments so that your monthly check is $4,500 before deductions.

75. SALARIES VARY BY FIELD. Philosophers make less than business school professors, who make less than law school faculty, all of whom make less than physicians teaching in medical schools. For some reason, people in mathematics do well. Exceptions occur in some institutions (usually state colleges) where salary is determined by rank (and step in rank). It doesn't matter whether your specialty is hospitality or nuclear physics.

76. ADMINISTRATORS USUALLY ARE PAID more than professors. Admittedly, most administrators were once professors who abandoned that calling. They claim that they should be paid extra to cope with the stress that comes from the many nasty things they need to do. Because they work for the entire year, their pay is based on 12 months. A $54,000 academic salary becomes $72,000 even before the bonus for administration. And, oh yes, they usually receive one month of vacation.

However, administrators, president or dean or functionary, are not tenured as an administrator. Administrators therefore must make their money now because they can (and generally will) be out on the street (or back teaching) if they make a misstep or become unpopular. For example, the optimistic estimate for the half-life of a dean of a business school is five years. As the present focus on accountability increases, administrator half-lives decrease (implying risks increase) and hence they seek financial incentives to accept the increased risk.

77. WORKING IN THE SUMMER. The three months "vacation" you receive can, in theory, be spent by you in any way you please. Go to the seashore or abroad, write a book, or work on papers needed for tenure. In practice, young faculty work during the summer for money to supplement the low salary they accepted (see Hint 36 on real pay). Teaching summer school, if offered to you, usually is paid miserably.

Notes

1. In some schools, the contract is for 10 months.

9

LIFE AS AN
ACADEMIC

HINT 108: NEVER, NEVER BECOME A DEPARTMENT CHAIR. . . .

NOW THAT YOU KNOW ABOUT FINDING A JOB, the things you need to do to reach full professor, and the financial aspects of academia, we turn to the things that affect your day-by-day life. This section, and the subsections on being an institutional citizen, on becoming a department chair, and on dealing with grievances should help you understand the life you are preparing to undertake.

78. BAD DEANS CAN MAKE your life miserable. Don't assume that because the half-life of deans is five years (Hint 76), you can outlast them. Get out your résumé.

79. NEVER, EVER CHOOSE SIDES in department politics. The side you are on expects your support because its members know they are right. They will give you no reward for it. The side(s) you are not on will remember forever.

80. NEVER TAKE A JOINT APPOINTMENT, particularly as your initial appointment. The chairperson of each department will assume that the other chairperson will take care of you. Each department will assume it owns at least three-fourths of you, Furthermore, at raise, promotion, and tenure times, each department will judge you only on the papers you published in its own discipline.

81. SECRETARIES (NOW OFTEN CALLED "ADMINISTRATIVE ASSISTANTS" in keeping with the escalation of titles in society) are a scarce resource. Treat them as such. Most universities pay secretaries below market wages and expect them to gain psychic income from the academic environment. They often work in physical spaces you would not accept even as a graduate student. (We estimate that the chance a secretary works in an office with a window is approximately one in three.) By any standard, they are an exploited class. If you develop a good relationship with them, they will work miracles for you. They know every arcane administrative procedure needed to get things done. They can say nice things about you to people who matter in the department. Remember, however, that if they don't like you, they can kill your reputation.

82. TEACHING ASSISTANTS AND GRADERS. After years of being one, you know that research assistants and graders are perceived as the sherpas of academe. Their role is to be as inconspicuous as possible and carry the burdens as their professors climb the mountain of knowledge. It is unfortunately true that many young professors rapidly adopt the same attitude. Doing so is actually a mistake.

83. GRADING. Your students learn from the feedback they receive, and graded papers are an important feedback tool. Thus, you need to pay attention to which answers are considered correct and what criteria are used for grading. In the case of examinations, you should grade papers personally rather than delegating the job to a teaching assistant, if you are assigned one. The examination is a form of communication, of feedback, between the student and you. You find out what the students really know and what principles and concepts did not get through to them.

84. SIMILARLY, YOUR RESEARCH ASSISTANTS require supervision. Having them take data for your key experiment or survey instrument is appropriate, but the final responsibility for their output is yours. You need to know what they are doing and how well they are doing it. Treat them with respect and show them that they are valued. One way to do this is to be generous in sharing authorship with them when they make contributions to your research. In short, you must teach them the research art. Remember that disgruntled graders or research assistants need not get mad at you; they can easily get even.

85. PHYSICAL PLANT. Like the computer center and other service operations, you must deal with the physical plant department. The people in physical plant are the ones who provide the services that you take for granted: moving furniture or fixing heating or changing lightbulbs. Your first contact will typically come when you move into your office. In our experience in a number of universities, we found three typical characteristics:

- Many people in physical plant are highly skilled craftspeople who can do wondrous mechanical and electrical things. They know about things you never learned.
- Physical plant is working on many jobs simultaneously. Although your job is the one that you think is most important, it is only one of many, some of which are emergencies.
- Physical plant charges for its services. Often it needs to charge quite a lot because the job is much more complex than you realize. Be sure you have a big departmental budget available before you call physical plant.

86. JOIN THE FACULTY CLUB, if your school has one. You will usually be taken there at some time during the interview process. If it is at all typical, it will seem like a cross between your undergraduate dining hall and the stuffy clubs you see on BBC mysteries. If you look around, it may seem that it is the haven for the superannuated.

Don't be deceived. The faculty club can be one of your most important assets. It is a place where you can meet with colleagues without interruptions of telephone or students. People always feel better when they eat and will often tell you things they would not otherwise reveal. In other words, it is a good place to keep up with what is going on. Being seen there by the older faculty in your department can be a plus because it shows you want to fit in. You will be surprised to find that you can actually have occasional intellectual discussions with people from other disciplines. It is also a good place to impress visitors and students. The food, of course, will rapidly become tedious.

87. OFFICE HOURS ARE SACRED at some institutions. You *must* be in your office at the times you promise. In other schools, they are merely advisory. Know what the situation is at your institution and follow the local custom. In general, you are required to provide times certain for students when they can contact you. Making appointments is one way. If you do make an appointment, be sure to keep it. A reputation of not keeping appointments is as bad as one of not replying to e-mails.

88. SABBATICALS. The best fringe benefit that a professor receives is the sabbatical. It is not, repeat not, a vacation. Here are some hints on what you should do on your sabbatical:

1. Do productive work.
2. Use the time for reflection and for getting into new things.
3. If at all feasible, leave town and never show your face at the institution during the sabbatical. If you appear, you will be put to work.
4. Stay in touch with your dissertation students (you can do this by e-mail or by meeting the students off campus).

5. When your sabbatical is over, write a good report on what you did so the administration will give you another one the next time you are eligible.

Always apply for a sabbatical as soon as you are eligible. Most institutions do not allow you to accumulate the time for future use. If you wait an extra semester or two, you will never get the accumulated time back.

89. MAINTAIN COLLEGIALITY. Collegiality is a difficult term to define. It involves maintaining good social relations with the people in your department and in related departments around campus. If everyone in your department has coffee in the lounge at 10:00 each morning, be there even if you only drink mineral water. If colleagues ask you to cover a class or review a draft of their latest paper or serve on a doctoral committee they chair, do it. The web of obligations is two-sided and you will receive reciprocal favors over time. Collegiality is one case where the commitments, even though they take away from your research time, yield positive results. Don't be perceived as a loner or a misanthrope, particularly by the senior faculty.

90. BE AWARE THAT AS AN ACADEMIC you are a public person. Your students spend 40 hours or more a semester doing nothing but looking at you while you talk. This experience makes an indelible impression on them. You will find that several years later when they approach you and call you by name they will expect you to remember them. You, of course, usually will not. Their appearance and dress will be different. The important point is that your behavior in public places is noticed when you least expect it.

91. WE FIRMLY BELIEVE THAT PEOPLE should be free to express their views on public issues, whether the views are mainstream or not. But understand the associated career risks. The conventional wisdom that academics are free to say what they please may well be the reason why you chose your career. However, our observation of what really goes on leads us to a different take for untenured faculty. No matter what your position on an issue, be it popular or unpopular, for or against the environment, for or against gun control, once it becomes known there will inevitably be people who are on the other side of that issue. They will consider your position a form of bad judgment and they will hold it against you. Remember that people in academia have long memories. Even if everyone in the department publicly espouses the same cause, you cannot be certain what position each one takes privately. Consider something as seemingly safe as excoriating the oil company whose tanker caused the latest oil spill. Your colleagues could be the people who consult with that company, who are writing its corporate history, who have a nephew who works for the company, or who own 3,000 shares of the company's stock. Of course, once you achieve tenured full professor, the situation changes.

92. ATTEND INVITED LECTURES. When world-class people are invited to lecture, be they in your field or not, be sure to attend if at all possible (and definitely if they are among the 100 important people in your field as discussed in Hint 2). When you were in graduate school, intellectually important people would come to campus to give seminars and to spend a day or two with faculty and students. Often, they became memorable events in your life. You would attend just to see who these people were. Now that you are a faculty member, don't feel too busy to attend such sessions. Even if the topic doesn't seem interesting to you, go. What you will hear, if you listen carefully, is how they think about the world, how they approach problems, and how they work on them. Often they will change your perspectives about your own areas of teaching and research.

The same advice goes for attending meetings of your professional society. At big meetings, the leaders in the field (the 100 of Hint 2) will present papers, give keynotes or tutorials, or participate on panels. Make a point of attending their session even if it means missing a paper or two in your own area. These meetings offer you the opportunity to observe these people, meet them, and to tune in to how your own work stacks up against what they are doing. Often you will be surprised that your work matches or exceeds what they are involved in. Both authors of this book experienced conference goers walking into a multi-paper session just before they were scheduled to speak and leaving as soon as they finished talking.[1] It is a common phenomenon at meetings and one you should participate in.

If you are at a small school, you can help bring people to campus to lecture. For example, many professional societies maintain visiting lecturer programs in which people volunteer to visit campuses. Look at the lists and arrange for your department to invite some of them. If you live in a metropolitan area that includes other institutions, get on their mailing list and find out who is coming to visit there. Advertised lectures are open to the public. If you belong to a local chapter of your professional society, work with the program committee to bring interesting people to its meetings.

Remember, lectures are a way to keep up with your field at almost no cost.

93. Letters of reference. The time will come when you are asked to write letters of reference for your students to help them obtain a job or get into graduate school. Requests will come both from students you treasured and from students you barely remember or whose name and face you couldn't put together on a bet. A simple

"Jane Jones attended my class last spring and received an A minus" won't do. You should try to personalize as much as you can. Ask for a résumé if the student has one. We sometimes find it useful to ask the student to write a draft we can start from. It's a win-win situation and a teaching moment. The students think about how they want to present themselves, something few students do on their own. Even better, you are saved from composing a complete personalized letter from scratch. You save time and you write a better letter of reference.

94. SERVING AS AN EXTERNAL REVIEWER. As you advance in your career, someone at another college or university will ask you to write an external review for a person up for tenure or promotion. The first time you receive one of these requests you will probably be flattered and think it a high honor to be considered sufficiently knowledgeable or important to undertake the task. Unfortunately, it is not an honor but a ritual that schools go through because they don't believe what they see in front of their eyes. They've lived with the candidate for five or more years. Yet for tenure and promotions, they ask for evaluations from people who at best met the candidate briefly once at a national meeting.

Why do they do it? On one level, they are celebrity hunters, little different than paparazzi. The more well known the evaluator, the better. On another level, they do it because that is the way it was always done and it might, just might, tell them something damaging that they did not know before. Better to be safe than sorry.

Some schools allow the candidate to supply a list of people who should be consulted, some (but not all) of whom will be chosen. That's supposed to make it fairer. The wise candidate includes personal friends in such a list. Such evaluations are window dressing because they only yield letters of praise and contain no real information.

The key question asked of the evaluator is often: "Would you grant tenure to (or promote) this individual at your institution?" The question dodges the issue because what is required at your institution is not what is important at the requesting institution.

Evaluations are considered a free good. Deans and committee members don't value the work that goes into the recommendation because they don't pay for it. Yet hundreds of dollars are spent by your school for your own time and that of the secretaries involved. The requesting institution often doesn't even write a thank-you letter, much less let you know the outcome. Your own institution gives you no credit for such work because it is done for somebody else.

Unless you are well established or the request is completely outside your field, you can't really avoid the task. Usually it includes reviewing attached papers and books (you may not be interested in) and writing an evaluation that answers a set of questions. Fortunately, the amount to be written is not extreme. Our experience is that letters of under one page and much over two pages are considered negatively (you're hiding something significant by saying too little or too much). You should be careful even in a two-page letter. If you think the candidate deserves promotion or tenure, be sure not to write a balanced account that discusses positives and negatives. A hint of something negative can be seized upon by a committee member or administrator who is opposed as a reason for saying no. Evaluation letters don't change the politics of the situation.

Your Digital Life

Although some of your more ancient colleagues still resist the personal computer after more than 25 years, you will be immersed in things digital. This section discusses many ways the digital world changes your academic job. Many of the hints you find in this section will be known to you. However, we believe that some will be new and useful. So pick and choose among them.

95. LEARN THE IDIOSYNCRASIES of your institution's computer center. You have a high probability of having to deal with the computer center, even if you are in the humanities. Although a computer center is a service organization, it is sometimes staffed by people who are not service oriented. This attitude is particularly true of computer center directors. Treasure the director who is service oriented. If not, your frustration level will be high every time you approach the center. Some directors are super security conscious. Like the librarian who believes that the best place for a book is on the shelf, such directors want to keep you from actually using the center because you might not follow their arbitrary rules.

96. ELECTRONIC MAIL EXTENDS your reach and range. The Internet is almost universal. If you know where a scholar teaches, Google will lead you to his or her campus's Web site where you can find the person's e-mail address, the department, and more just by typing the name into the institution's search engine. Thus, you have a global address book at your fingertips. Similarly, you can reach your students outside class and they can reach you outside office hours (but see Hint 99). Amazingly, the Internet is free, but unlike the telephone no directory comes with it.[2] Start the habit of electronic communication when still a graduate student. As you meet or contact people, obtain their electronic address and add their name to your e-mail's address book. You'll be amazed at how quickly you will build a directory of people who can give information and advice. It is part of the networking that we so strongly recommend. The community you connect with will help you, and you will help them.

97. E-MAIL HAS ITS DOWNSIDE. First you must deal with spam, viruses, and spyware. Spam is mail that tries to entice you to spend money for things you don't need. Viruses are "malware" that try to damage your computer or hijack its use for another's gain. Spyware comes in a variety of guises, such as tracking your actions on the computer, in the hope of learning about you. As we write, spam is increasing and its practitioners are becoming more sophisticated about avoiding interdiction. For example, you will be offered great wealth from Nigeria if only you put up a substantial amount of "earnest money." People will try to get you to open attachments that contain viruses or ask you to provide personal information, such as your credit card, Social Security, or bank account numbers and passwords, so they can rob you. Recognize that university computer account names are easily stolen and your name may be used to bamboozle others. Fortunately, many schools subscribe to electronic communications security services, such as Postini, that quarantine or remove most malware and spam. However, these services don't deal with spyware, which sends information about you back to the sender. Ask for both virus and spy protection for your computer at the office and buy such protection for your home computer. They are wise investments. Most important, know about the problem and be careful.

98. IT IS EASY TO JOIN lots of e-mail lists that will bring you interesting news of your field from both inside and outside academia. Like alcohol, e-mail lists should be used in moderation or not at all. Too many, and you waste your morning going through your e-mail rather than paying attention to teaching and research.

99. YOUR STUDENTS LOVE E-MAIL. It is a way for them to communicate with you directly whenever they feel the urge, day or night, rather than waiting for class or coming during office hours. They expect an instant response from you, whether it is midafternoon or three o'clock in the morning. Some expect you to act as if you were their slave. It is a bad student habit that can easily get out of hand.

Some faculty members we know tell their students that they answer e-mail only sporadically.

100. KEEP ABREAST OF NEW WAYS of using the computer. Wikis, blogs, instant voting, and course management software are four examples we discuss here. Your students will often know about new computer tools before you or even your computer center people do, and they will expect you to know about them and use them.

- Wikis and Wikipedia. The term *wiki* comes from Hawaiian and it means to do things quickly. A wiki is software that creates a public text forum that can be edited or added to by anyone with access to the Internet or to a school's local Intranet. Wikis are extremely simple and easy to use by nontechnical people. For example, each student in a class can contribute material to a written discussion, submit homework, or receive information from the instructor or your teaching assistant. Using a wiki for homework discourages plagiarism among students because each student's work is seen by everyone else in the class.

  Wikipedia (http://www.wikipedia.org) is a large wiki that contains an electronic encyclopedia, much larger than the *Encyclopedia Britannica*, freely available on the Internet. It is a marvelous place to obtain an introduction to almost any topic. Two caveats: (a) Because of its open authorship, Wikipedia can and does sometimes contain errors, and (b) your students may be tempted to plagiarize Wikipedia in their papers. It is wise to check Wikipedia to catch copying.
- Blogs. The term *blog* comes from Web log. It refers to Web sites maintained by one or more individuals who create a diary with the most recent entry shown first rather than last and with the intent of being publicly available rather than private. Blogs are usually interactive so that readers can make comments. Blogs can be on any subject, such as the material being covered in a

class, politics, or simply personal records. You, as a faculty member, can maintain a blog for comment by your students and vice versa.

- Instant feedback and voting. Relatively low-cost devices are on the market that allow feedback and voting during class. These devices, often called "clickers," give students a few choices that are recorded by the instructor's computer. In a typical device, using wireless transmission, the instructor displays multiple-choice questions on a screen about what was just discussed in class and asks students to select one of the options. The statistics on the student answers give the instructor instant feedback on the question so that the instructor can see whether they understood the material. If they did, you can proceed. If not, you can expand and reiterate until they get your point.

- Course management software. Course management software is used by faculty and students to improve communication on what is required in the course and on its content. For a given course, students can find the syllabus, texts required and recommended, assignments, messages from faculty and other students, chat rooms for studying jointly for exams, and take exams. They also can be directed to material that expands on the course. Among many on the market, Blackboard and Moodle are perhaps the largest, most available management software packages used by colleges and universities. If you are moving to a new campus, find out which course management software is used there. It is prudent to obtain training on the software before you arrive, as you may be expected to start using it from the first day of class.

101. MEETINGS AND DIGITAL PUBLICATIONS. Become familiar with the digital aspects involved in proceedings publishing and presentations at meetings. They're all done by e-mail. Even if you don't write for the electronic journals in your field, you will still use e-mail to

- submit your papers (and resubmit revisions)
- receive review comments
- receive letters of acceptance
- receive and send back proof copies

and more. You will find it easiest to set up separate folders for each paper. Also, use identification numbers and/or dates for each version you create so you can keep track of what is current and what is old.

102. INTERLIBRARY LOAN IS QUICKER and more efficient than it used to be. For example, you can order reprints of journal articles that are delivered to your e-mail inbox. But you need to know the full reference to get what you want. We recommend that you not give up going to the library to browse through the stacks. You will find articles and books there that you didn't know existed.

103. USE DIGITAL LIBRARIES IF THEY ARE AVAILABLE in your field. Many professional organizations, particularly in the sciences, offer full paper access to all their publications, past and present, via the Internet. These libraries are not for free. Typically you must be a member of the organization and pay an annual fee. However, these libraries are so vast and searchable, that the fee is well worth it whether you are primarily a researcher or a teacher.

Institutional Citizen

As a member of the academic community, you are a citizen of the institution. You have obligations to the institution just as it has obligations to you.

104. GET TO KNOW THE DEVELOPMENT PEOPLE in your school and support them.[3] At most institutions, one or more people on the development department's administrative staff are charged with obtaining endowments and other gifts, maintaining relations with alumni, and so on. Skilled, interactive development offices can help in obtaining outside funding for you, for your department, and for students, all of which improves your quality of life. Be careful, however; development offices can be horribly inept. Their people are usually underpaid and in this world you get what you pay for. Many are fund-raisers who know nothing about the academic enterprise or what you do. You will be educating them over and over. You may need to team up with colleagues to get people replaced who are extremely bad.

105. BE RESPONSIVE TO THE ALUMNI OFFICE just as you are to the development office. For many alumni, their college experience is the highlight of their life and the old school tie is one of the few things they can flaunt. They like to hear good things about their school because it makes their degree more valuable. If you are asked to write something for the alumni bulletin or give a speech, do it. Alumni can support their old department in a variety of ways. If they know you, they can support you from the outside at moments of crunch.

106. WHEN YOU DO SOMETHING NOTEWORTHY let your school's public relations department know and ask them publicize it. When you publish a book, win a prize, get elected to a professional society office, or do something in the community, get public relations into the act. It is one way for a lot of your colleagues across campus to find out what a wonderful person you are. (They may even remember it at promotion time!) It also lets you brag to your chairperson and to the people in your department without being obnoxious about it.

107. THE FACULTY SENATE IN MOST INSTITUTIONS provides a forum. People are elected to it, usually by their department or their school. If elected, it provides a way for you to communicate with the higher levels of administration on matters important to you and to your department. Election also increases your visibility. Be aware, however, that Faculty Senate work can eat up a large amount of your time. Our advice, therefore, is that if you are asked to run, do so, providing you are tenured and as long as the senate is not a collection of malcontents who are ignored by the administration.

Department Chair

Department chairs will seem to be lofty people to you, having a job you think you should aspire to. It's not quite all wine and roses.

108. NEVER, NEVER BECOME A DEPARTMENT CHAIR, even an acting department chair, unless you are a tenured full professor. Yes, it will reduce your teaching load. Yes, it will give you visibility. Yes, you will be the first person contacted by an outside firm seeking a consultant. No, it will not confer power on you. The job carries with it some onerous burdens. First and foremost is that most department chairs do less research and publish less while in that position than they would as a faculty member. Thus, you are producing less portable wealth per year (Hint 39), and you are reducing your chances for tenure or for promotion. The service you perform does not get you tenure. Don't feel flattered if the job is offered and you are pressured by the dean to accept it. What is really going on is that the dean has no other viable candidate who is willing to do it. If you must accept, realize that you are in the same bargaining position as a new hire. The dean wants you badly. Use the opportunity to obtain something in return. If you are untenured, accept the job subject to the condition that tenure is granted in the next academic year; if you are an associate professor, insist on a promotion to full professor. Be clear beforehand that you will resign the chair's job if the agreement is broken and, if it is (as is often the case!) follow through. As the advertisement says, deans operate on the principle of, "Promise them anything but give them . . ."

109. BE AWARE THAT THE POWERS of a department chair are few. One of us wrote down the following seven absolute powers he had at a particular university:

- the right to attend meetings of the department chairs with the dean
- the right to chair meetings of the department
- the right to interview candidates for secretary
- the right (subject to a few side conditions) to select which classes he or she would teach and at which times
- the right to approve (or disapprove) student petitions
- the right to greet outside visitors to the department
- the right to resign as chair

110. YOU WILL SPEND A CONSIDERABLE AMOUNT of your time solving problems brought to you by your faculty colleagues. The faculty will want you to obtain goodies for them (space, computers, research money, reduced teaching loads, and on and on). On the other hand, the dean will want you to act as a first-line manager whose main role is to keep the bastards down so they cause no trouble.

The job is best characterized by a line from Gilbert and Sullivan's *Gondoliers*:

> But the privilege and pleasure
> That we treasure beyond measure
> Is to run on little errands for the Ministers of State!

111. As a faculty member you will learn a lot about bad management by observing the various chairpersons, deans, and higher administrators. You will feel that any dolt could do better than they do and you will often be right. At some point, however, management may become real for you if you are asked to become a department chair or an associate dean. Now you must provide leadership and avoid the traps that your predecessors fell into. Management is a discipline that you can study and learn. Those people in the Business School really do know something and what they know about is leadership. Like teaching, leadership is a learnable art.

112. If you do become department chair, recognize that most students who come into your office do so while in crisis. They are unhappy about a grade. They want to be exempted from a course or an examination. They need to explain that they did not cheat even though their term paper was identical word for word to one submitted by another student last year. You are the end of the line for them. You cannot throw them out. You need to listen and be firm while at the same time being sympathetic. It takes a strong stomach and a feeling for people.

113. Despite the foregoing caveats, being a department chair does offer redeeming social values. If you have a vision of where you think the future of the department lies, you can use your moral suasion as chair to move people in the direction you believe right. Notice we use the term *moral suasion,* not power. You need to develop a constituency for your ideas. In academia, Theory X management (I tell, you do) does not apply. Japanese Theory Z management (nothing happens until consensus is reached) is the appropriate model.

114. IF YOU ARE DEPARTMENT CHAIR, don't stay in the job too long. You become a victim of your past decisions. You become locked into doing what you did before, whether it is still the appropriate thing to do or not. Fortunately, unlike industry, you can keep pace if you step down and work for someone who previously worked for you. When you step down, don't second-guess your successor(s) on every little point. They, like you before them, need all the help they can get.

Grievances

There comes a time in the life of both students and faculty when they whine about the injustice of it all. Some realize that grievance procedures exist and follow them. As an academic you need to know about these procedures.

115. YOU MAY, AT SOME POINT in your academic career become involved in a student grievance. We are a litigious society, fueled in part by a supply of lawyers and in part by demand for equal treatment under the law. Fortunately, most universities and colleges provide grievance procedures to handle disputes. We estimate that the chance of your being involved in a student grievance sometime during your academic career is 50%. Typically these disputes are over grades, results of examinations, acts of cheating, and the like. Sometime they are the result of delusions by students about their abilities. Other times they are the results of behavior on your part that a student perceives as insulting or demeaning.

116. THE LAST SEVERAL YEARS SAW THE GROWTH of sexual harassment as a basis for complaint. You may wind up as the originator or the recipient of such a complaint. The source may be a student, a staff member, or another faculty member. Remember that harassment complaints can lead to litigation in court. Your institution may or may not be supportive. If it isn't, you can wind up spending large amounts on lawyers and court fees. The best strategy is preventive. Here are a few things you can do to protect yourself:

- Know and obey your institution's rules on harassment.
- Know what the procedures are for the offended party.
- Never meet with a student of either sex behind a closed door.[4]
- Never use language or examples that are sexually offensive.

117. RECOGNIZE THAT FACULTY RARELY VOLUNTEER to serve on the grievance committee. It is not pleasant duty. The result is that members are often appointed to this committee when they are not appropriate for other current vacancies. They do not have the experience or skills of judges or dispute professionals. Like most judicial proceedings, the results contain a certain element of chance. Committees often fudge the outcome, particularly if the grievance is framed in a "she said, he said" form. Thus, even if you are completely in the right in a dispute, try to avoid using this committee. Furthermore, as a young faculty member, avoid serving on this committee if at all possible.

118. YOU MAY BECOME THE GRIEVANT against your institution. Disputes can arise over such issues as tenure; sabbatical entitlements; teaching loads; outrageous treatment by department chairs or deans; salaries; discrimination because of age, gender, or ethnicity; and more. Most institutions offer a grievance procedure. The bad news is that many people will remember the incident negatively even when you win.

Dealing With Myths

When you talk with family, friends, and others who do not work in academia, don't be surprised to discover that they believe some of the standard myths about professors. The following hints deal with two of them.

119. MYTH 1: "I envy all the free time you have. You mean you actually get paid a full salary for working only 12 hours a week?" They may even tell you that old joke. Question: What does a professor say at the end of the work week? Answer: Thank God it's Tuesday.

Actually, most professors work well over 40 hours per week, and that includes not only the time on campus but also the time at home in the evenings and on weekends. If your department offers courses to students who are employed full-time, you will be on campus some nights until 9:00 or 10:00 p.m.

120. MYTH 2: "All professors are political Leftists. Our universities are controlled by radicals and liberals."

Most surveys show that the majority of professors are either conservative or middle of the road. You will discover certainly that when it comes to changing their own behavior, your colleagues are unusually conservative and move very slowly. They follow Frank H. T. Rhodes's sardonic assertion "Never, under any circumstance, do something for the first time."[5]

Notes

1. Of course, some headed for the exits even while we were speaking.

2. Americans used to scoff at the Russians because they did not publish telephone directories. They managed well without them and we seem to be doing so without Internet directories.

3. Development is an old-fashioned term. Many of the larger schools use the fashionable name *advancement*. Ironically, most advancement campaigns begin with a retreat for faculty.

4. Some of our colleagues believe this advice is too stringent. They argue that when a student requests privacy it calls for a closed door. We disagree. Privacy can be achieved as easily by walking with the student to a quiet food area or public space.

5. Rhodes is president emeritus of Cornell University. He made this statement at the 1997 opening of the Keck Graduate Institute. He referred to it as The Cardinal Law of Academic Governance.

10

DIVERSITY

HINT 121: Although you may hear that universities are leaning over backward to hire women and minorities, such cases are exceptions and are rare.

THE DIVERSITY THAT EXISTS IN THE general population in the United States does not yet apply to the American professoriate. This statement is not surprising, given that most of the faculty currently serving in academia were hired at a time in the previous century when diversity was only talked about but was not practiced. Diversity, in our view, reflects the presence of both women and men and includes people whose ethnic roots may be from Europe, Africa, Asia, and the Western Hemisphere. To simplify our discussion, we will concentrate on women and people of color. However, our points are applicable to all groups.[1, 2]

All the hints in this book apply to new faculty members but perhaps more so to women faculty and faculty of color. Whereas portions of this book take a lighthearted view of many aspects of academe, in this chapter we are deadly serious. To the authors, diversity is an important goal and one that is still far from being realized. We quote research results and we try to dispel some of the myths that currently surround the subject.

The reality of the situation is given in the following quotation:

> *The search and hiring process continues largely unchanged. The lack of diversity on search committees continues to limit the potential for introducing new perspectives to the process of evaluation.*
>
> *The climate for faculty of color in institutions remains uncomfortable and difficult, regardless of the circumstances under which the individual was hired.*[3]

121. ALTHOUGH YOU MAY HEAR that universities are leaning over backward to hire women and minorities, such cases are exceptions and are rare. Based on a review of the data we were able to find and on the experiences of junior professors we know, these claims are not supported.

In response to increasing concern over the lack of diversity in universities, some improvement has occurred, but it has been at the margins. For example, between 1993 and 2003, the percentage of underrepresented minority faculty "grew from 6.8% to 7.2% within the University of California system" and grew roughly from 6% to 8% nationally at four-year institutions.[4] Do not expect that a 0.4% increase (if you seek employment in the University of California system) or even 2% represents a sea change in the college or university culture. The University of California employed 8,200 tenure-track faculty in 2005.[5] So we are talking about a net increase on the order of 30 to 40 positions for the University of California system over a 10-year period. For four-year colleges, the full-time instructional faculty was 626,000 in 1993.[6] A 2% change would indicate about 13,000 positions. Although this number is nontrivial, it translates on average into a total of 10 to 15 positions over 10 years at an institution.

122. WHAT SHOULD YOU DO if you fall into the underrepresented minority category? Diversity varies greatly among institutions. When considering an offer, and even when making an application, try to find out whether the institution you are considering as your future intellectual home shows a genuine openness and commitment to supporting and mentoring all junior faculty, including women and people of color. A massive study of attempts by universities to diversify their faculty concluded, "Campuses with greatest gains had explicitly connected their . . . efforts to their educational mission and had implemented multiple strategies to improve the recruitment and selection process with regard to [underrepresented minority] candidates."[7]

123. IN ADDITION TO TRYING TO ASSESS how open and supportive your future institution is, also assess, to the best of your ability, your future department colleagues and your future dean. As we said in Hint 78, don't assume you can outwait a bad dean.

Given a Hobson's choice, it is better to take a position at the institution of your second choice if it has a supportive culture (even if its academic reputation is slightly lower) than at your top choice if you conclude you will encounter sexism and/or racism.

124. An analysis of roughly 700 faculty searches concluded that underrepresented minority faculty are more likely to be hired at predominantly White institutions when the job description "explicitly engages diversity," "an institutional 'special hire' strategy is used," or when an "ethnically/racially diverse search committee" is referred to.[8] This research provides clues to help you sort through job possibilities. Check if the advertisement for the position stresses diversity and look at the ethnic makeup of the search committee.

125. THE CLIMATE FOR WOMEN IN ACADEMIA has improved more than the climate for people of color, but we still are a long way from full equity. Women still encounter extra obstacles and chillier climates at each step up the academic ladder. Yes, women are now presidents of Ivy League schools. Yes, women dominate the numbers in some fields. However, the firestorm over remarks by the former president of Harvard University, Lawrence Summers, about the possible genetic inferiority of women for work in the sciences and engineering highlighted how far we still must go in academia.

On some campuses women belong to formal support groups. For example, on one campus a "Female Faculty Forum" was created as a reaction to perceived nonresponsiveness from the administration. The female faculty meets as a group once a month to discuss policy issues and politics at the university, to share concerns, and to support one another.

126. To learn about the current situation, study the growing literature by women and minority scholars about the academic world. For example, Gail Thompson and Angela Louque published *Exposing the "Culture of Arrogance" in the Academy: A Blueprint for Increasing Black Faculty Satisfaction in Higher Education* (Stylus Publishing, 2005). They combine statistical analysis of survey data from a sample of African American faculty members with interview data. The picture they paint is not always pretty. When asked about the most difficult aspects of life in the academy, the survey respondents cited the low number of faculty of color and the racial climate. Like other faculty members, they also mentioned issues we addressed in these hints: time for research, time management, time for course preparation, and the teaching load.

Notes

1. Our definition of diversity applies to faculty, students, curriculum, and research topics. In this chapter, we concentrate on faculty, particularly newly hired faculty.

2. In this chapter we consider underrepresentation in predominantly White, coeducational institutions. We do not explicitly consider an important part of academia, the historically Black colleges (e.g., Morehouse) or historically women's colleges (e.g., Scripps).

3. D. G. Smith, L. E. Wolf, B. Busenberg, and associates, *Achieving Faculty Diversity: Debunking the Myths. A Research Report of a National Study* (Washington, DC: Association of American Colleges and Universities, 1996).

4. J. F Moreno, D. G. Smith, A. R. Clayton-Pedersen, S. Parker, and D. H Teraguchi, *The Revolving Door for Underrepresented Minority Faculty in Higher Education: An Analysis from the Campus Diversity Initiative* (San Francisco: The James Irvine Foundation, 2006), p. 2.

5. M. A. Mason, A. Stacy, M. Goulden, C. Hoffman, and K. Frasch, *University of California Family Friendly Edge: An Initiative for Tenure Track Faculty at the University of California*, 2005, http://ucfamilyedge.berkeley.edu/ucfamilyedge.pdf

6. *Digest of Educational Statistics* (Washington, DC: Institute of Educational Sciences, U.S. Department of Education, 2004).

7. Moreno, et al., *The Revolving Door*, op. cit., pp. 7–8

8. D. G. Smith, C. S. V. Turner, N. Osei-Kofi, S. Richards, "Interrupting the Usual: Successful Strategies for Diversifying the Faculty," *Journal of Higher Education* 75, no. 2 (2004).

11

ON WRITING

HINT 127. LEARN HOW TO WRITE CLEARLY.

Teaching, research, and writing are the three activities that academics engage in most. Writing manuscripts—research papers, books, or class notes—requires specialized skills. Here are some thoughts about writing. We discuss publishing what you write in chapter 12.

127. Learn how to write clearly. Some graduate programs do their best to stamp out this skill, persuading doctoral candidates that a ten-syllable word is better than a two-syllable word. Reviewers are more likely to persevere to the end of your journal submission or your grant proposal if they can easily follow what you say. They are also more likely to give you a favorable review. If all else fails, use the style of these hints and the writing tips given in Appendix C.

128. Learn the fine points of English. With multiple degrees in hand, you are assumed to be an educated person. Writing and speaking mistakes turn off your students, reviewers, and the editors of journals.

If you need help, buy a copy of *Fowler's Modern English Usage* and William Strunk Jr. and E. B. White's *The Elements of Style*.[1, 2] Read them. When in doubt, consult them. As we point out in Hint 127, a well-written paper is more likely to be accepted than a poorly written one.

For example, you should

- know the difference between assure, ensure, and insure, and between affect and effect.
- recognize that criteria is plural and criterion is singular

To help you with your writing, Appendix C presents a series of simple hints to make your prose sparkle. Absorb them now. Go back to them whenever you finish a draft for submittal and apply the principles as you edit the manuscript.

129. BE SURE TO SPELL-CHECK (and grammar-check and fact-check) your work. Your degrees certify you as a literate, educated person. Grammatical or spelling errors in a résumé or in an article submitted for publication turn off reviewers who are making judgments about you. For example, in a résumé sent to one of us as an outside reviewer for tenure we found the following: "My research activities has centered on . . ." and a reference to the journal *Group Decision and Negotiation* wound up as *Group Decision & Negation*.

130. PLAGIARISM IS A CARDINAL SIN. You would fail a student who plagiarizes on a term paper and you would excoriate a colleague who fails to reference someone else's intellectual capital. However, it is perfectly all right to plagiarize yourself, within limits. Experienced authors use portions of their previous work when writing a new manuscript. This is part of the rich-get-richer phenomenon.

For example, one of us begins writing a new book by creating a text file containing relevant excerpts from his previously published books and articles. In one case this file contained 70 pages. This strategy provides a wonderful psychological boost that generates momentum without writing one new word; your typical new book already contains more than 50 pages!

Of course, once the full book text is completed, rewritten, and edited, the 70 pages will wind up being 12 to 15 reused pages. But the discarded pages served their psychological purpose.

131. LIMIT SELF-PLAGIARISM. Under some circumstances you can appropriately cite one of your old findings in a new publication, if it is relevant. In fact, you can recycle some text from one of your previous manuscripts in a new one. But do not base too much of the new manuscript on text you published previously.

132. SIMILARLY, UNDER DREW'S RULE of Conference Redundancy, you can cite a previously published finding, or one you presented earlier at a conference, in a new and different context. But don't overdo it. Here is a good rule of thumb: If you found a correlation (a number between 0 and 1), multiply it by 10. That's how many years you can still discuss it.

For example, one of us discovered and reported in 1975 a correlation of 0.91 between (a) the prestige of graduate mathematics departments and (b) the rate at which their faculty published in the discipline's most highly cited journals. He was asked to discuss this finding at several conferences. He accepted the last such invitation in 1984.

133. ONE OF THE MOST USEFUL THINGS you can develop is a pool of research references stored in your computer.[3] You will use the same references over and over as you do research, as you write papers, and as you teach. You will add to this list as you read new articles and books in the literature. We personally recommend the software called EndNote[4] although other similar kinds of software are on the market. Software for references contains three useful features:

- It provides a standard form for entering references so that you remember to include all the necessary data. Separate forms are provided for each type of reference (books, articles, newspapers, Internet URLs, etc.).
- It automatically converts the format to the reference style of the journal to which you are submitting. Lots of different styles

are available. Since you may be sending an article to several journals sequentially before it is accepted (see Hint 4), this automated feature saves you hours of drudge work in converting reference formats.

■ It provides space for including abstracts and notes so that you can record what the reference is about for future retrieval.

134. IF YOU CONDUCTED A THOROUGH literature search for your dissertation, you will never need to do one again as long as you write in the same area. If you write in an adjacent field or on an adjacent topic or want to include the latest reference, your cycle time for the literature search is much, much shorter. Remember too that your students or graduate assistants will perform some of the slogging that needs to be done.

Notes

1. R. Allen, ed., *Pocket Fowler's Modern English Usage* (New York: Oxford University Press, 2006).

2. W. Strunk Jr. and E. B. White, *The Elements of Style,* 4th ed. (New York: Longman, 1999).

3. Be sure to keep a copy of this list separately—for example, in a removable drive or in printed form. Computer storage is known to crash occasionally.

4. *End Note* is published by the Thomson Corporation, http://www.endnote.com/

12

ON PUBLISHING

HINT 143: PUBLISH EARLY AND OFTEN.

A T SEVERAL POINTS ALONG THE WAY, we stressed the need for you to publish if you are going to survive in a research-oriented institution. In this section (and the subsections on journals and on book publishers that follow), we present what you need to know about the publication process. Also, go back to Hint 4 (Drew's Law) that tells you every good paper can find a home.

135. SUBMIT YOUR PAPERS (other than those you know are stinkers) first to the best journals in the field. Work your way down the list if a paper is rejected. Many articles rejected by a poor journal were later accepted by a leading journal, so you might as well start with the best. It is easier to follow this rule if you are thick skinned.

Two additional factors should affect where you place a journal on your "go-to" list (not all journals make this information public): (a) the percentage of submitted papers the journal accepts, and (b) the length of time the journal takes to review a submission.

136. WRITE MOST OF YOUR ARTICLES for refereed journals. Papers presented at meetings get you funds to be a world traveler. However, even if refereed, conference papers don't really count for tenure, promotion, or salary raises.

137. AVOID WRITING INTRODUCTORY TEXTBOOKS when you are not tenured. You can make a lot of money, although many of these books wind up taking so much time that you would be financially better off if you had worked for minimum wage at McDonald's. Most tenure committees think of them as moonlighting, not scholarly productivity.

138. RECOGNIZE THE DIFFERENCE between writing the first paper on a subject and writing the nth one. Writing the first paper requires a special knack for originality that few people have. A first paper usually is not very deep, but it creates enough of an impact that others follow your lead and write deep, scholarly works. The advantage of the first paper is that it is always referenced, giving you a long list of citations. If you are fortunate enough to have the knack, you will need to market your output carefully. Journals (and reviewers) look for the tried and true. Journals, after all, publish almost exclusively on subjects they published previously. Tenure and promotion committees will read the paper and say that it is trivial because they read the more careful papers that others wrote later based on your idea. It has been our observation that people who write first papers possess a different set of skills than those who write the nth ones and should leave the writing of the nth papers to someone else.

139. WRITING THE NTH PAPER MEANS that $N - 1$ papers on the subject were written before yours. Although you need not cite all of them, you should cite enough of them so that authors of previous papers will be selected as reviewers. (One of the secrets of the journal editor business is that editors find reviewers by looking in the citations for names of people they know.) You may, however, be unfortunate enough that the paper is sent to someone for review whom you did not cite. If so, the reviewer will comment that you failed to include the citation, which, of course, is a dead giveaway of the reviewer's name.[1]

140. IN WRITING THE NTH PAPER, make your contribution to the issue clear. It may be a carefully done experiment or an elaboration of the theory or a synthesis and interpretation of previous work. Whatever it is, be explicit in claiming it in the paper. The reviewers need to be convinced that the manuscript contains something new that merits publishing.

141. AS AN AUTHOR, YOU DON'T HELP MATTERS if you take a long time between receiving reviews and submitting the revised manuscript.

142. REVIEWING IS A SCARCE RESOURCE and it is important work. You will want your work reviewed quickly. You should offer the same courtesy to others. Don't be too busy to review, and turn your reviews around quickly

143. AS THEY SAY IN CHICAGO, publish early and often. N matters, even though $N + 2$ is required for tenure (see Hint 1). Begin writing for publication while you are still in graduate school. Data show that people who publish while still in graduate school usually continue to publish at a faster rate after they graduate than those who didn't publish while still a student. Furthermore, published papers and monographs help you get your first job.

144. YOUR DISSERTATION IS A PUBLISHING ASSET. You should receive a return on your investment for the time and money spent in creating this asset. In the humanities, it should lead to at least one book or monograph. In the social sciences and the sciences, at least two papers should result. We recommend that, as a rule of thumb, one of these papers should be single author, the other joint with your major adviser. Your major adviser put intellectual capital into the dissertation just as you did, and the joint publication is one way you can repay the adviser for the hours spent poring over your work and helping you over the tough intellectual hurdles. You should agree on this arrangement with your adviser before starting on your dissertation. Avoid advisers who insist on joint authorship on all papers that result. They are exploiting you.

145. THE LITERATURE SEARCH YOU PERFORMED for your dissertation is a treasure trove of information. It should be the foundation of a survey article on the field. And the world desperately needs more survey articles. Unfortunately, although only a few journals (e.g., *Computer Surveys*) accept such articles, you receive little credit for them in tenure and promotion reviews. You will be rewarded more for adding one little new data point to the literature than for a brilliant synthesis of that literature (unless your name is Arnold J. Toynbee). You can, however, transform a literature review into a meta-analysis, which is a systematic, statistical aggregation of previously published research findings. Such a paper carries more cachet with tenure committees, and the statistics are not difficult.

146. INCLUDE SINGLE-AUTHOR PAPERS in your portfolio. Review committees wonder about people who always publish with someone else. Did they do the work or did they ride the coauthor's coattails? Were they the first author? If you must coauthor, pick people whose names follow yours alphabetically and then suggest that your name really belongs first. (Choosing the order by drawing lots, as was done for this book, is not recommended.) If you are unfortunate enough to be named Zyzygy, go to court and get it changed.

147. COAUTHORING A PAPER WITH A SUPERSTAR increases your visibility and associates you with his or her reputation. However, be careful which papers you coauthor. If the idea is yours, the superstar will likely get most of the credit.

148. RECOGNIZE THE DELAYS in publishing. In fact, you face long, long delays. In this hint we estimate the delays in journal publication. For books, the total time is usually much longer. Let's assume you've written your first article and printed out a copy that is ready to send off to the top journal in the field. If you expect that this brilliant piece will appear in the next issue or, at the latest, the one after that, we have a bridge to sell you in Brooklyn. Let's assume that your paper is so good it is accepted without a request for even minor revisions. Even in this unusual case, the pace of publication is extremely slow. To help you understand the time delays, we've created Tables 12.1, 12.2, and 12.3 that show you the work flows. (If there was ever a process that needs reengineering, it is this one!)

Note that Table 12.1 shows that your paper is not yet mailed to a reviewer and a month has passed.

If you add these times up you see that the typical time to get an answer is about six months (Table 12.2). We are very generous in this best-case assessment. In real life, longer periods are not at all unusual.

At this point you can claim publication if the paper is accepted. If revision is required, you need to add the time you take to revise,

TABLE 12.1
Work Flow in Periodical Publishing

Step	By	Time Required
1. Produce copies of the manuscript, prepare cover letter, and e-mail.	You and your department staff	1 week
2. Acknowledge receipt (publishers get a lot of submissions).	Editor's office	1 week
3. Decide who is to review.	Editor	1 week to 4 weeks*

*Some editors work in batch mode. They let manuscripts pile up for a while and then work on a group of them over a convenient weekend when it is raining or snowing outside.

TABLE 12.2
Time to Decision

Step	By	Time Required
4. Manuscript sent to two reviewers	Editor's staff	1 week
5. Review time	Reviewers	4 months
Most reviewers are senior people who are asked to review a lot of manuscripts. One colleague of ours totaled up the number he reviewed in a particular year and found it was 73. A good reviewer turns a submission around in four weeks; a poor reviewer can take six months. We won't even talk about the lowlifes who take a year. We estimate the median time to be three months.	Note that it is equally likely that a reviewer will take more or less time than the median. Remember that the time required for the review process is determined by the *slowest* reviewer.	The probability that both reviewers take less than the median time is 0.25; thus the review time for your manuscript will probably be longer than the median.
6. E-mail to editor	Reviewers	1 week
7. Accept/reject decision and e-mail to author on decision	Editor	1 week

the time the reviewers spend agreeing that the revisions meet their standards, and exactly the same delays in mailing and writing e-mails as for the original draft. We leave it, as the mathematicians say, as "an exercise to the reader" to compute the delay if one, two, or three revisions are required.

But, you're not the proud possessor of your name in print yet. There are a few more steps involved, as we show in Table 12.3.

Many of the numbers in the printing process are quite broad. For example, if a journal is published quarterly, an extra three month's

TABLE 12.3
Production Time for Accepted Journal Manuscripts

Step	By	Time Required
1. Manuscript is put in the queue for publication.	Editor	None
2. Depending on the backlog, the manuscript is sent to the compositor.	Editor	1 month
3. Manuscript is typeset.	Printer	2–4 weeks
4. Manuscript (now called "the galley") is sent back to you for final proof.	Printer, editor	2 weeks
5. The galley is proofread and mailed back to editor.	You	2 weeks
6. If submitted to a journal, manuscript is assigned to an issue.	Editor	No time
7. Manuscript is printed and the issue is bound.	Printer	1 month to 2 years depending on backlog
8. Issue is mailed out. You receive an author's .pdf copy of your article.*	Printer, editor	2–4 weeks

*Authors used to receive a copy of the complete journal issue or a printed copy even if they did not order reprints. Most publishers today merely send you a .pdf copy of the printed version via e-mail.

delay may come just from your being the $N + 1$st article for an issue of N articles in a quarterly.

Journals

You rely on journals as outlets for your work. Your relationship with a journal can also include becoming an editor or a reviewer.

149. DON'T ACCEPT THE IMPRESSIVE TITLE editor-in-chief or department editor of any publication early in your career. Journal editing takes time. Don't get involved at the editorial level until your career is well launched. At all costs, avoid editing struggling newsletters, special-interest publications, and the like.

150. Do, HOWEVER, SERVE AS A REVIEWER for journals, particularly top journals. Treat this job seriously. You will see much junk being submitted and appreciate why some journals reject 80% or more of their submissions. You will develop an aesthetic for what is good and what is not. You will correspond with some powerful people (see Hint 2). When you do get a good paper to review, you will receive much earlier knowledge of an important new development. The information gained is worth more than the time you take reviewing.

Book Publishers

Although the Internet and multimedia are here, the foreseeable future will still include textbooks and monographs. Book publishers are like honeybees. They bring intellectual pollen that you need for your classes. Publishers are outlets for your books (but see Hint 137 about the trade-off in writing textbooks).

151. PAY ATTENTION TO THE BOOK PUBLISHERS' representatives who come into your office. They are a valuable source of information. These reps have two missions: (a) to flog the books their company issues and (b) to send intelligence back to the home office. They will be pleased to send you complimentary copies of the latest mass market elementary textbooks in your field. If your field is French, you can obtain many shelves of freshman- and sophomore-level French books. You can also obtain copies of books directly linked to specific courses you teach. It is a little more difficult (but not impossible) to obtain complimentary copies of books in your research area. There's always the chance that you will adopt. Don't, however, simply look at the reps as a source of freebies. Use them to find out what is going on in the book market. Sound them out on whether their firm is interested in a book manuscript you have under way. Their response will usually be positive. Ignore that. Just make sure that they get the word about your forthcoming manuscript back to the editors at the publisher's headquarters.

152. SELECTING A PUBLISHER involves trade-offs. With a large publisher that issues many books in your field in a year you gain the advantage of mass marketing and advertising. Large publishers employ reps who visit campuses. However, these reps are given many books to push and their commissions depend on the number of books sold. As a result, they concentrate on freshman and sophomore texts for required courses. Furthermore, since they receive the same commission no matter which book is adopted, they have little incentive to sell a particular book. Thus, you run the risk that promotion of your book will be lost among the many others with similar titles being offered by that publisher. Small and specialty commercial publishers and university presses give you much more individual attention. You can judge whether they are a good fit for your book by looking at their publications list on their Web site, the mailings you receive from them, the advertisements in your professional journals, and the recommendations of your peers. Before signing a contract, make sure that (a) your publisher will have your manuscript peer reviewed, and (b) the publisher you chose "counts" with your field's tenure committee. Under *no* circumstances publish with a vanity press, that is, a publisher that charges you for publishing your book.

153. GET TO KNOW THE MAJOR EDITORS of the book publishers in your field. The best place to meet them is at the book exhibits associated with your annual professional conference. You will find that some of them know absolutely nothing about your field, not to mention your subject. Avoid working with such editors because they will treat your work as a commodity, like pork bellies.

Note

1. Some argue that you should cite everyone who ever wrote on the subject. This approach is not desirable and often not feasible. If the area is well published, you can never be certain you found every (obscure) reference, your list of references would be extremely long, and too long a list may well be held against you. Better to take your chances that you found the relevant references and cited them.

13

PERSONAL CONSIDERATIONS

Hint 157: Learn time management.

THE HINTS IN THIS SECTION refer to your actions as an individual.

154. LEARN NEW THINGS OVER TIME. Universities are notorious for not spending money on faculty development. Universities assume that, because you earned a PhD, you learned all you ever need to know. They are not consumers of their own educational product. Actually, you know the most about your field the week you take the Preliminary Examination for the PhD. Thereafter, you tend to specialize and learn more and more about the narrower and narrower subfield you work in. But, it is unfortunately true that fields change over time. Some subspecialties are mined out and new results become ever more difficult to obtain. Other subspecialties make rapid strides that require you to learn new methodologies and become aware of a flood of literature. Some new technologies, such as computer-based retrieval, come along and change the research skills you need. If something new is important to your research, try to get your department to spring for some education. It may be a short course offered by the leading expert in the field or a tutorial offered at a professional meeting. If it is sufficiently big, arrange for your next sabbatical at one of the centers where the new knowledge is being developed.

155. ONE DAY THE PHONE WILL RING and you will be asked by a lawyer to be an expert witness. It looks like easy money. The attorney will tell you that all you need to do is help prepare the technical material in your specialty (which is fun) and to appear in court to swear to your findings. An ethical attorney will offer you a fixed fee or a fixed rate rather than ask you to bet on the contingency that your side will win. It isn't really that simple. The legal culture is different from the culture in your field. You will need to bridge the two-culture gap; the lawyers won't and can't. You will teach the attorneys about your field. If you are a scientist you will blanch at the low level of proof offered in court cases and you will be appalled at the level of statistics being used. When you do get to court, you will find you spend much of your time waiting around. Waiting is not bad; you are getting paid a premium for every hour spent in court. When it does come time to take the stand, your side's lawyer will lead you through a carefully rehearsed set of questions. Then the fun begins. The other side's lawyer will cross-examine you. The operative word is *cross*. Their lawyer will try to find inconsistencies in what you said. The opposing side will try to twist your words to be favorable to its client. The other attorney will try to impugn your expertise, your honesty, your veracity. You can come out with a very jaundiced view of jurisprudence. The whole process will eat up a large chunk of your time. If you are an untenured professor, remember that the income carries with it a large opportunity cost (see Hint 173), the time lost working on your research. The work done for a court case is almost never the basis of something publishable. Tenure committees view being an expert witness as public service or consulting income, not professional work no matter how complex the case. If you do become a regularly employed expert witness, your initial choice of sides can quickly become permanent. If you are hired, say, by plaintiffs seeking psychic pain and suffering awards in auto accident cases one day, you will not credibly be able to represent an insurance company defendant the next.

You should conduct your analyses with integrity and report your findings with candor. This ethical approach may cost you some expert witness income. If the attorney doesn't like your findings from your background work, he or she won't ask you to testify in court. And the attorney may not hire you for the next case.

156. DON'T BE A PENNY-ANTE THIEF. It may be awfully tempting to put personal correspondence in official envelopes, to use department secretaries to type your private letters, or to make personal long-distance calls. Don't use department funds to buy software or journal subscriptions that are designed to support your consulting practice. To paraphrase Abe Lincoln, you can get away with some of it all the time, and you can get away with all of it some of the time, but you can't get away with all of it all of the time. Don't develop a reputation of being someone who only takes not gives, of not having ethical respect for your colleagues or your institution.

157. LEARN TIME MANAGEMENT. First, finish reading this book. Then determine your work priorities. Then try as best you can to match your time commitments to those priorities. Alan Lakein's *How to Get Control of Your Time and Life* is a marvelous, short guide to time management.[1]

Some examples:

- Ask your students to take notes when they meet with you and to send you a memo within 24 hours that records what was said. The memo allows you to check whether they understood you and you them. It also releases you from copious note taking.
- Some professors do their research and writing in the morning and all other tasks, including teaching and committee work, after that (or vice versa).
- Use e-mail but don't become an addict.
- Learn to say *no*!

One of our colleagues, who published well over 30 books in his career, advised: "If you write only a page a day, that's a book a year!"

158. COMPLETION TIME. No matter how long you think it will take to

- write a paper based on your research
- see the paper you just submitted in print
- complete a research project
- prepare a new course
- prepare for a session of a course you gave previously,

it will always take longer.

The wide-eyed optimists always think the task will be completed on time.

The mildly realistic optimists think the task will take their estimated time plus 10%.

The pessimists understand that the delay is at least 50% on average.

Corollary: Even if you add the above delay times to your estimate, it will still take longer than that.

Notes

1. Alan Lakein, *How to Get Control of Your Time and Life* (New York: Penguin Signet, 1974).

14

FINAL THOUGHTS

HINT 159: ONCE YOU ESTABLISH a reputation, people will pursue you.

159. THE RICH GET RICHER holds in academia as well as in society in general. Once you establish a reputation, people will pursue you to do things, such as write papers, make presentations at prestigious places, consult, and so on. To reach this position you must earn your reputation. If you do reach it, remember that fame is transitory. You must keep running, doing new things, to keep the demand going. So, once you become one of the 100 (Hint 2), you will gain rewards, but you will also work furiously to keep your riches. Those who read these hints will want your place!

160. FINALLY, A COLLEAGUE OF OURS once told us: Treat students as though they are guests in your home.

It is simple, sound advice. If you carry nothing else away from these hints, remember this one.

15

CONCLUSION
AND ENVOI

HINT: PROFESSOR IS THE BEST JOB on the planet.

N THESE HINTS WE DESCRIBED LIFE based on our own experiences (and mistakes) as well as on observing our colleagues at universities throughout the country. We did not try to quote the many learned studies of academe by academics nor paint a picture of the ideal world that academe should be. For example, we believe, as most aspiring academics do, that teaching should be more respected and rewarded than it is, but we know that in many institutions it is a necessary but far from sufficient condition for tenure.

These hints apply in today's academic job market. We hope that the coming demographic reversal will provide the impetus to change the system so that this book will be read as an artifact of an ancient, more cynical age.

When we started writing these hints, we found previous attempts to encapsulate similar wisdom. In typical academician's fashion, of course, we did not read them. We invite readers to send us their own rules so we may tell future students about them in future editions. We will, of course, give you credit for your suggestions.

ENVOI

In this book, we are frank, cynical when necessary, and hard-nosed. We provide you with the best career advice we can. We hope this approach does not leave you with a jaundiced view of academia. We consider professor to be the best job available on the planet. Universities are wonderful, and occasionally transcendent, places to work. Most, but by no means all, of the great intellectual and scientific advances since the Enlightenment were made in universities. It is both a thrill and an honor to contribute to knowledge through your own scholarship. Furthermore, you may well conclude that the most valuable and meaningful work you do is teaching and mentoring students. You are given the rare opportunity to guide the expansion and development of young (and older) minds and ideas over your entire lifetime.

Enter this exciting world, but with your eyes wide open.

Appendixes

Hints 194 & 197: Addictions . . . Meditation. . . .

APPENDIX A

The Dissertation

WE PUT OUR THOUGHTS on the dissertation into this appendix because many of our readers have already completed graduate school and some are well into their careers. If you pick up this book while still a graduate student, we think these hints about the dissertation will be helpful to you.

161. FINDING A DISSERTATION TOPIC is not as easy as it looks. In fact, for many students it is the most difficult part of their dissertation work. (Not only that, but many students erroneously believe that defining a topic is the easiest part of the dissertation. "If I'm having so much trouble with the easiest part of this task, how will I ever finish?") Some students go to a professor they want to work with and ask for a topic. Usually they wind up desperately unhappy because they don't "own" the topic yet are condemned to work on it. Often these students spend the rest of their life as ABDs.

162. DON'T ASSUME THAT IF YOU are having trouble defining a dissertation topic that the entire dissertation process will be that arduous. Once you define the topic, you are in problem-solving mode, and most people do well in solving a problem once they know what the topic is.

163. PUT A LOT OF EFFORT INTO WRITING your dissertation proposal. The proposal provides two important payoffs:

1. It usually provides one or more chapters of your end product, the dissertation.
2. It is a contract between you and your advisory committee on what you must do to receive the degree. In general, if you do well what you promise in the proposal, the committee should sign the final document. If, because of circumstances, you cannot accomplish all you set out to do, you have the basis for negotiation.

164. IF LITTLE OR NOTHING IS WRITTEN on your dissertation topic, don't assume that an abbreviated literature review is acceptable. Dissertation committees are used to a minimum-sized review and will insist on it. If only three previous papers even touch on your subject, reviewing just them is not considered an adequate literature search. Furthermore, the new data you expect to obtain, even in a specialized topic, can affect a lot of intersecting fields. Those fields should be identified. In short, a literature review not only discusses what is already done and why, it also points out the areas where your work has implications.

165. BE SKILLFUL IN WHOM YOU SELECT for your dissertation advisory committee. The worst possible approach is to pick people because they are famous in their field. Rather, recognize that the role of the advisory committee is really to advise and help you. Therefore, choose people who can help you over the rough spots. If your dissertation is experimental and requires expertise in two fields, pick an expert in each field and someone who knows about experimental design and statistics. When push comes to shove (and it will at some time while you are working on your dissertation), the persons you need will be there to help you because they made a commitment to you. Simply hoping that the expert will contribute time to your problem without being on the committee can prove to be naive.

166. IN DOING A LITERATURE SEARCH, use the "chain of references." Begin with one or two recent articles (a survey article helps!). Look at the references that are cited. Then read those publications that seem apropos and look at their reference lists. Some things will pop out often. These are usually (but not invariably) the classics in the field that you *must* reference. Proceed from reference to reference until the law of diminishing returns takes over.

167. COUPLE YOUR LITERATURE SEARCH (typically chapter 2 of your dissertation) closely with the discussion of results and the conclusions (typically chapters 4 and 5). You may find that as your dissertation progresses, some parts of your literature search are really irrelevant to your research. In this case, you should be ruthless. Despite the brilliance of your prose and the long, tedious hours you put into creating the material, you must delete these pearls. Of course, you should save the work as part of your file of references (Hint 133) so you can use it over and over in future publications.

168. THE RISK OF "NOT SIGNIFICANT." When you select a dissertation topic and write a proposal, be it qualitative or quantitative, you confidently expect to obtain significant results. Significance involves two dimensions:

1. The results are important to the field.
2. The results are statistically significant or produce new insights and understandings.

It is perfectly possible that your results don't show the effect you predicted, or the analysis does not meet standard statistical significance tests, or you were not able to find a second or third site you promised in your proposal. This risk, although usually small, is there in all dissertations. It's a form of the promise-performance gap.

What do you do if it happens to you? In almost every case, you shouldn't give up or quit your pursuit of the PhD. Follow plan B. Yes, you must convince your adviser (and your committee) that you needn't start over. But you obtained a lot of data during your work. The data can be used to show, for example, that:

- the methodology you used is correct, but the effect is not there with this methodology on the sample used.
- with a meta-analysis based on adding your results to others, existing theory is stronger (or weaker) than thought previously.

APPENDIX B

Outside Income

PROFESSORS, BEING HUMAN, look to maximize their income, no matter how large or small it is. Opportunities exist for earning more from the university through teaching overloads or teaching summer sessions or executive or noncredit courses, among others. However, most schools treat you for such work the same way they treat adjunct faculty. They pay as little as possible because they are maximizing their income.

This appendix is concerned with outside income from consulting and from grants and contracts. We've talked previously about other sources of income such as writing textbooks (Hint 137) and/or serving as an expert witness (Hint 155).

169. CONSULTING MEANS DOING WORK for an organization for compensation, as opposed to professional activities that are contributions to your field but for which you should not expect to be compensated. Examples of professional activities include reviewing papers submitted to journals, reviewing grant proposals, and serving on or chairing committees of a national or local professional association. In consulting, you are a hired hand, asked to give advice about what to do. It is typically paid on a time basis.

170. CONSULTING INCOME IS FOUND MONEY. It comes to you episodically. Do *not* plan on future consulting income, under any circumstance, when constructing your family budget. Even if you can trace a steady $5,000 or more per year from consulting over the past six years, you are not guaranteed that you will earn any consulting income next year unless you have a contract in hand. Even then, corporate fortunes change and you can be terminated. We recommend that you use your consulting income, after you receive it, either to buy large, durable items (a new TV or computer or refrigerator) or to save it for a major vacation or buying a house.[1]

171. DON'T GO OUT AND SPEND the consulting checks you receive until you put money aside to pay the taxes on it. Consulting income is taxable, like all other income, and can put you into a higher tax bracket. Your employer has to file a 1099 form and the IRS is superb in using that form to find you if you don't report the income. Fortunately, you report your consulting income on a special form (Schedule C) that allows you to deduct legitimate expenses incurred in generating the income. We strongly recommend you consult a tax specialist about how to prepare Schedule C. A good tax specialist who knows what can and cannot be deducted will often save you a considerable amount and is worth the investment.

172. GRANTS AND CONTRACTS. Receiving an academic salary for nine month's work seems to leave you vast amounts of time to undertake lucrative additional work, such as consulting. It usually does not work out that way. Your teaching responsibilities often spill over into summer. More to the point, even if you are a full professor, you may need that summer for research and writing. The best way to earn extra income while moving toward academic goals is to secure grants and contracts. Most federal agencies and other funding organizations that provide research support for summer work, usually pay the equivalent to two month's salary (i.e., two-ninths of your academic salary). Some may provide three month's support. Some, but not all, research schools will allow you to work one day a week during the regular year for pay by outside sources.

173. BOTH JUNIOR AND SENIOR PROFESSORS sometimes slip into doing extensive summer teaching, usually at reduced rates. It is a way to earn needed extra income by doing something you know how to do. Recognize that you incur what the economists call an *opportunity cost* associated with this income. In summer teaching you close out other opportunities, especially research and writing opportunities that could advance your career. However, if your school offers substantial summer research grants, go for them.

174. BE AWARE THAT PAYMENT you receive through your school is usually considered regular income. You may not be able to use Schedule C to report it or to deduct the associated expenses.

175. PRO BONO CONSULTING. If you are a beginning professor, the chances are you are struggling to make ends meet. Later in your career, you should consider doing some consulting jobs pro bono, that is, for free. In the past few years each of us has advised organizations pro bono. For example, we worked pro bono advising a non-profit conflict resolution and peace organization about how to evaluate its educational activities, advising a religious group in another country about founding a college, and leading a team of students to improve an orchestra's database.

176. CONSULTING RATE. If you are being considered for a consulting job, you will be asked what your consulting rate is. Fees for consulting vary by discipline and by client, Therefore, it is difficult for us to suggest generic rules that always work. Nonetheless, here is a best practice guideline for your daily rate for business clients:

1. Take the annual pay in your 9-month contract and divide it by 165, the standard number of working days in 9 months. That calculation gives your daily income from your institution.
2. Multiply the number you just computed by 2. The factor of 2 indicates that you must be paid more for your knowledge than just your regular pay and it also takes care of deductions such as Social Security and Medicare taxes.

For example, if your nine-month salary is $66,000, dividing by 165 yields a daily income of $400. Multiplying $400 by 2 results in $800/day (= $100/hour) as your consulting rate.

Some additional considerations:

- Charge not-for-profit organizations a lower rate than you charge profit-making organizations. They have less money and usually are not able to afford you at your full rate.
- If you are really a world expert in your field or if your school's salaries are in the lower quartile of academic salaries, you can, of course, charge more than the amount you compute from the above method.
- If you can, find out what other consultants are charging the firm. It's a delicate question to ask and some people will inflate their actual rate. Nonetheless, don't be bashful about it. If you ask too much you lose a client; if you ask too little, you'll kick yourself for it later.
- Should you charge for travel time in addition to travel cost reimbursement? Sometimes you must travel quite a distance to

the organization where you are consulting. It is better to address this issue explicitly when you are negotiating the consulting agreement. We tend not to charge for travel time (but do charge for travel expenses) if we are not working on the client's project while travelling. Some consultants charge half their rate for travel time.

177. WARNING! YOU CAN'T TEACH ELSEWHERE for outside money if you are on the tenure track. Universities and colleges do not let you moonlight at another school without permission. It's a conflict of interest. The specific permission rules vary from place to place, but they are there. We know of one case where a tenured faculty member in an eastern U.S. university took a second appointment in another university within driving distance. When found out, he was asked to resign, and he did.

Note

1. As a consultant you are running a business. One of the risks of business is that you, like a plumber or a painter, don't always get paid what you and your client agreed on.

APPENDIX C

Writing Hints

THIS APPENDIX IS AN EXPANSION of Hint 128. It contains tips that will help you in writing and editing your manuscripts, be they your dissertation, papers, a book, or monographs. These tips are based on our experiences. Furthermore, one of us spent eight years of his youth as a technical editor. As indicated in Hints 127 and 128, good writing increases the odds that your submission will be accepted.

We use the term *paper* in what follows to represent all forms of publication. You may find that specific journals and publishers have idiosyncrasies of their own. If so, follow them rather than us.

178. DON'T TRY TO EXPLAIN YOUR FIELD or subfield from first principles. You are not writing a textbook for undergraduates or an article for your alumni magazine. You can assume that your reader is familiar with the field in general and knows all that. Do explain what the reader needs to understand you.

179. AVOID PASSIVE VOICE. Passive voice is dull and pedantic. Typically, in passive voice, you use the verb first and then give the subject. Active voice makes your work interesting to read. In active voice, the subject performs the action given in the verb. For example:

> Passive voice: The girl was bitten by the dog
> Active voice: The dog bit the girl
> Passive voice: Statistical tests were conducted to check the validity of the hypothesis.
> Active voice: Statistical tests checked the validity of the hypothesis.

180. AVOID SHOULD AND MUST. These prescriptive words assume you are in a position to give advice and that you found the only way to do something. Such is rarely the case. Business and policy papers are particularly fond of this bad habit, although it also shows up in many other fields.

181. AVOID TOO MUCH BOLDFACE and italics. You **SHOUT** when you use bold and/or *italics* in your text. Bold and italics used sparingly are a great help when you present something really important. If you use them over and over, the reader starts ignoring them. Italics used the first time you define a term are OK. Similarly, you can put a term in quotation marks at first use.

182. YOU CAN RARELY BE BOTH "effective and efficient." The two words are used together by some almost as a mantra. You rarely achieve both simultaneously. Usually the best you can do is trade off one for the other.

183. DON'T GENERALIZE FROM a single case. You are limited to the results from that case and that case alone.

184. DON'T BE AFRAID TO USE numbered or bulleted lists. Don't try to put everything into straight text. You can wind up writing:

A method. . . . Another method. . . . Another method. . . . A fourth method . . .

It is a lot better to say:

The methods are:

1. . . .
2. . . .
3. . . .
4. . . .

Because a list breaks material up visually, it helps your reader follow you more easily.

185. USE FIGURES AND TABLES. Like lists, figures and tables break up the monotony of text. They make information easier to read and understand. Word processing programs usually let you create tables and draw simple figures.

186. LEARN TO USE STYLES in word processing programs. Microsoft Word and most other text programs contain features that make it easy to create different-looking documents. The journal you write a paper for or the book publisher will specify what format they want for submissions. Styles, built into the word processor, let you change the appearance of the document automatically to fit your requirements.

187. USE THE SPELL-CHECKER. Papers with spelling errors are often rejected out of hand. At the least they define you as either careless or illiterate, neither of which are desirable traits. Use your spell-check on the final draft. Be careful, however. It is quite easy to misspell the word you wanted and obtain a word that passes the spell-checker. For example, if you type *their* when you meant *there*, the spell-checker won't catch it.

After running the spell-check and making corrections, be sure to read the paper one more time from end to end (better still, ask someone else to read it as well) before you send it out.

188. PAY SPECIAL ATTENTION TO REFERENCES. Your paper's reviewers and your readers will note your references in text and turn to the list of references. Use the following tips:

1. Be sure your references are accurate. Be accurate in spelling names, dates of publication, journal name or publisher, and other details of a reference. Remember, an author of one of your references may review your paper. Think about the retribution if you spell the author's name wrong.

2. Reference what you quote. If you quote someone or some source, be sure to include a reference with full publishing information. If you don't, you can be accused of plagiarism.

3. Use multiple references when you synthesize several sources. Be sure to include references to all the sources you use.

4. Put dates on each URL.[1] It is OK these days to reference publications on the Web. When you do, give not only the URL but also its date. If you can't find an author, use "Anonymous." Put "Undated" in your reference if a date is not available. Be sure to include the date when you last accessed the Web reference.

5. Put references in a list at the end of your paper.
   Exception 1: Some journals require putting references in footnotes.
   Exception 2: Book publishers usually put references in endnotes.

6. When using a reference in text, follow the requirements of the journal. Examples of references in text:

Typical : "The results (Smith 1998; Smith and Jones 2000) . . ."[2]
Referring to a person by name: "As shown by Jones (2003), . . ."
Refer to one of several references by the same author in the same
year by adding "a," "b," "c," and so on to the year: (Smith 2004b)

189. ELIMINATE POOR WRITING HABITS. Here are some examples:

1. Avoid "there are," particularly at the start of a sentence.
   Example:
   Replace: There are three ways to obtain knowledge, . . .
   With: Three ways to obtain knowledge are . . .
2. Don't split infinitives. In a split infinitive you put one or more
   words between "to" and the verb. You can always write
   your way around a split infinitive.
   Example:
   Replace: To successfully manage knowledge, . . .
   With: To manage knowledge successfully, . . .
3. Do not use "etc." The reader does not know what you include
   in your et cetera. Readers often interpret etc. differently
   than you do. You can convey the same idea by using "including" or "such as."
   Example:
   Replace: ". . . text, voice, graphics, etc."
   With: ". . . including text, voice, and graphics."
4. Use "to" instead of "in order to." In most cases, particularly
   at the beginning of paragraphs or sentences, it is sufficient
   to say "to." You need "in order to" only when you mean
   "for the purpose of."
   Example:
   Replace: "In order to obtain knowledge, . . ."
   With: "To obtain knowledge, . . ."

190. WE USE THE TERM *BAD WORDS* to refer to words that cause the reader difficulty rather than words banned by the Federal Communications Commission from being broadcast. The words listed in the first column of Table C.1 are best avoided. The second column explains why. The words listed are representative. In general, if a word is a cliché or hyperbole or advertising or pretentious, replace it with a simpler word that conveys your meaning.

Note

1. URL stands for universal resource locator. It refers to the address of the resource on the Internet.

2. Some journals, such as those that follow the American Psychological Association (APA) style use the ampersand (&) rather than "and."

TABLE C.1
Bad Words

Word(s) to Avoid	*Reason*
Cutting edge	Cliché
Comprise	Comprise is used correctly when you say the whole comprises the parts (e.g., The Union comprises 50 states), but incorrectly if you say the parts comprise the whole (e.g., Fifty states constitute [or make up or compose] the Union, rather than they comprise it).
Discovered	Usually you are trying to say found or obtained. Discovery implies scientific discovery or, when the known world was smaller, finding a previously unknown territory.
Dramatically	Meaningless hyperbole. Do you mean a Noh play in which little happens, or a melodrama?
Ideal	Ideal means absolute perfection and is unprovable.
Incredible	Hyperbole.
It is important	Let the reader find out that something is important.
Perfect	Hyperbole. You can rarely prove perfection.
Perfect solution	Advertising hyperbole.
Recent	Academic writing is read for many years after publication. Something you published in 2007 is recent in 2008 but not in 2012.
Utilizes	Utilize is not a synonym for "use." Utilize means "to make use of" and sounds pretentious.

APPENDIX D

Your Health

Y OU MUST STAY HEALTHY to continue to hold down the academic job you sought for so long. Unless you keep your health, you can take ill, fatigue easily, or see your body decay. You can't guard against all health hazards (and you may inherit some from your family), but you can do some relatively simple things to maintain your health and stay ahead of your competitors. In this appendix, we offer hints about some of the problems you can encounter and what you can do to maintain balance and health. These hints are based on our experience. They are not intended as medical advice. We are neither physicians nor specialists in these areas.

191. MINIMIZE STRESS. Although we go into academia because we think it involves little stress, that's a legend that is not true. If you're junior and nontenured, you can expect that gaining tenure will be the most intense, stressful experience you will face in your entire career. You will be wondering whether you will be awarded tenure (it is never a slam dunk!). You'll be worrying about what you will do if you don't gain tenure. Furthermore, stress is not necessarily over once you receive tenure, although it is usually diminished. Of course, if you are a type A personality (impatient, insecure about yourself, competitive, aggressive, and rarely relax) you add your own internal stress to all that exists around you.

Stress also awaits you from outside academe:

- Money. For most professors, unless your family or you are really well off when you start your academic career you will face the problem of managing much more salary than you ever had as a graduate student. Although the salary may seem princely, you will still need to pay off your student debts and you will make considerably less than senior professors. The monthly check may never seem to go far enough. You must learn how to manage your money.
- Family Responsibilities. Most people receive their PhD between 25 and 35. If you don't already have a spouse or partner, these are often the years when you take on family responsibilities. These responsibilities are both emotional and financial. And they are on top of your nontrivial workload.
- Parents. As people live longer, your parents and grandparents will need care, and the responsibilities for that care can become yours.

The problems of money, family responsibilities, and parents don't go away even after tenure. Whether you are tenured or not, you will be affected by stresses within your institution. For example, a bad dean, a school in financial crisis, a department riven by politics, and outside political attacks on the university all contribute to stress. You will also find transient stresses, such as the potential repercussions from a student you failed or from the rejection of a paper you wrote that you thought was great.

192. Sᴛᴀʀᴛ ᴀ ʜᴇᴀʟᴛʜ ᴀɴᴅ ғɪᴛɴᴇss ᴘʀᴏɢʀᴀᴍ if you are not already involved in one, As academics, we take the written word seriously. Therefore, we suggest you begin by reading one or two of the many excellent books about health. Use well-established books, rather than the latest faddish one on magic exercises or fantastic diets. Talk with people in your school's health service or athletic department for specific recommendations.

193. Eхᴇʀᴄɪsᴇ. The establishment (public health officials and the medical community) is always after you to exercise regularly. This is a case where the establishment is right. If you're a couch potato who goes from the computer to the television and then to bed, find a half hour every day for some form of exercise, preferably aerobics.[1] For example,

- walk a half hour every day
- ride a bike
- jog
- swim

If you enjoy a form of exercise, you are most likely to continue the exercise program and to make it a lifelong habit. If you prefer, or need to stay disciplined, use a gym. Often your institution will offer exercise programs for faculty.

194. Aᴅᴅɪᴄᴛɪᴏɴ. We discuss three addictions here: smoking, drugs, and alcohol. Similar ideas apply to others addictions, such as the e-mail junkie.

STOP smoking immediately. We know this is easier for us to say than for you to do. Many stop-smoking programs are available. Shop around until you find a program that works for you. The cost of the cigarettes you don't smoke will more than pay for the program.

Drugs and alcohol. We won't go into detail on alcohol or drugs here. Suffice it to say that if you are addicted to either or both, it can:

- be successful grounds for firing you even if you are tenured. Obtaining another job will be difficult.
- reduce your research output, particularly for tenure.
- be nearly impossible to hide for long periods of time. You're a public person (Hint 90) who is observed by all around you. Some of your students and/or colleagues will pick up on it and word will get around.

195. Weight Control. Being overweight is the biggest factor above and beyond smoking that contributes to illness, fatigue, and decay. Obesity, and even less extreme forms of being overweight, lead to scary outcomes: high blood pressure, diabetes, sleep apnea, and some forms of cancer, to name just a few. Bookstores, libraries, and the world at large are filled with diet books and programs, from the Scarsdale Diet to Atkins to Jenny Craig. Unfortunately, many of these diets are fads and a lot of them aren't even effective. You are more likely to achieve weight loss over the long term if you follow a healthy diet and exercise regularly.

196. Studies of people who live to be quite old, (including those over 100) consistently find common diet elements. Diet recommendations could easily yield a book much larger than this one. Read one or two books on healthy nutrition. It is a complex subject and there is much to learn, for example, the importance and the different kinds of omega-3 fatty acids. For now, we'll simply list some of the consistent recommendations from the epidemiological, public health, and medical literatures:

- Eat a variety of fruits and vegetables.
- Limit your intake of red meat.
- Make sure you eat adequate protein.
- Eat nuts, beans, and whole-wheat bread.
- Limit your intake of complex and refined carbohydrates., for example, potatoes, pasta, rice, bread, and needless to say, cookies, candy, and soda.
- Drink plenty of water.

If your health plan pays for it (and even if it doesn't) it is helpful to consult a professional dietician occasionally.

197. MEDITATION. When we suggest meditation, we are not talking about a bearded man sitting cross-legged in front of a cave or high on a mountaintop. Male or female, you can meditate anywhere and it's not complicated. Do it for at least 10 minutes a day.

Why meditate? The medical literature increasingly talks about the cognitive, physical, and emotional benefits of meditation.

To meditate, simply sit in a quiet room, breathe slowly and deeply, and try not to obsess about your worries or the tasks on your to-do list. To drive such thoughts out of your mind while meditating, you will find it helpful to use a mantra, which is a constantly repeated phrase.

198. APPEARANCE. How you look and interact is observed continually (Hint 90). Fortunately, you're not expected to come to class dressed in a suit as though you were in a 1930s movie. You are, however, expected by your students and by your colleagues to be neat, not disheveled. For young faculty, it helps distinguish you from the students. It also helps if you are thought of as a person who smiles, not frowns.

As you age, your appearance will be affected by your health. For example, as a person of the book, the computer, and student papers, you depend on your vision for your livelihood. It's no shame for an academic to use glasses (or contacts) rather than squinting. As you head into middle age, you will inevitably become far-sighted. Don't do as one colleague we know does and keep pushing menus farther and farther away from your face. Rather, obtain reading glasses (even if you do purchase them at the local drugstore).

Hearing is lost a little at a time. For males, in particular, the high frequencies go first. If you've spent a lot of time at rock concerts or at pistol ranges, your hearing is likely affected. The symptoms show up in class. For example, you find yourself asking students (particularly students who speak softly) to repeat what they said more loudly "so everyone can hear." What's really going on is that you're becoming less effective in class, and sometimes even receive poorer teaching ratings.

199. INSURANCE. When we wrote this hint in mid-2007, most colleges and universities offered medical insurance to their full-time faculty as a fringe benefit.[2] It's almost always a better deal than policies you can buy on your own. Yes, in the first years out of graduate school, you'll use a lot less of it than your older colleagues and it may seem a bad deal. Furthermore, in many cases, adding your spouse and kids to your policy will cost you more than your own insurance, sometimes a lot more. If you're married with a working spouse who is also eligible for health insurance, take the coverage from the plan that is lower in cost. Recognize, however, that premiums by themselves are not an indicator of what is best. For example, different plans involve different copayments you make every time you use the insurance. Study what is offered and then make a choice.

Under any circumstance, don't remain without coverage. A serious health disaster can wipe out you and your family financially.

Your institution may offer a minimum amount of life insurance at little or no cost. If it's free, certainly take it. If the cost is minimal think hard about it. If you're the main breadwinner or a parent, even a little life insurance will be a great help if you get hit by a car crossing the street.

Notes

1. According to the *Oxford English Dictionary*, *aero* is from the Greek meaning "air" and *bic* is from the Greek word *bios* meaning "life." The benefits of aerobics include reducing stress, weight control, improved cardiovascular and muscular fitness, increased flexibility, lower cholesterol, and improved sleep patterns.

2. If you're an adjunct, you probably don't receive health insurance or life insurance. Although you may not be able to get an increase in the pittance that adjuncts are paid because the rates are uniform across the department or the college, you may be able to negotiate some health insurance. Try it.

ABOUT THE AUTHORS

DAVID DREW (david.drew@cgu.edu) and PAUL GRAY (paul.gray@cgu.edu) (the order of the names under the title was chosen by lot) are professor of education and professor of information science, respectively, at Claremont Graduate University in Claremont, California. You can find out more about them by going to http://www.cgu.edu/pages/388.asp and to http://www.cgu.edu/pages/2237.asp

MATTHEW HENRY HALL is a professional cartoonist whose work appears regularly in *Inside Higher Education.*